Key Stage 3

Maths

Ages 12–13

D0532989

Sheila Hunt

survival GUIDE

Letts Educational
Chiswick Centre
414 Chiswick High Road
London W4 5TF
Tel: 020 8996 3333
Fax: 020 8996 8390
Email: mail@lettsed.co.uk
Website: www.letts-education.com

First published 2001
10 9 8 7 6 5 4 3

Text © Sheila Hunt 2001

All our Rights Reserved. No part of this publication may be produced, stored in a retrieval system, or transmitted, in any form or by any means, electronic, mechanical, photocopying, recording or otherwise, without the prior permission of Letts Educational.

British Library Cataloging in Publication Data. A CIP record of this book is available from the British Library.

ISBN 1 84085 637 8

Letts Educational Limited is a division of Granada Learning Limited, part of Granada plc.

Edited and typeset by Cambridge Publishing Management

Designed by Moondisks Limited

Maths

Book 2 Ages 12-13

Introduction

What does starting Year 8 mean for you when it comes to maths?
Could any of these be you?
• I did well last year, but I'm not sure I can do the same in year 8.
• I'm in a high set for maths, and I want to keep it that way.
• I found maths really hard in year 7, and I'm dreading it this year.
• I really want to move up a set in maths.
• I'm hopless at maths, but I'd like to be better at it.

If you recognised yourself in any of those comments, then *Letts Key Stage 3 Maths Survival Guide Ages 12–13* is for you. It takes you through the topics that you are likely to meet in year 8 and revises some of the areas which many students may have found difficult in year 7. There are plenty of worked examples and exercises – all with answers – and the many 'Tactics' and 'Red alerts' will help you to tackle new topics with confidence, whilst avoiding those common mistakes which most of us make only too easily.

The number network

If you used Book 1 from this series, you may recognise the number network. The Book 2 version has a few extra connections to guide you through the coming year. If you haven't seen the number network before, don't panic. It's for reference only, and you are not expected to learn it! The number network is a quick way to check up on the skills you need before you tackle a new topic or process. You can't, for example, solve ratio questions without some knowledge of fractions. The number network shows you which areas you need to know before you tackle something new, and also just how far that newly-acquired skill could take you.

Have a good trip!

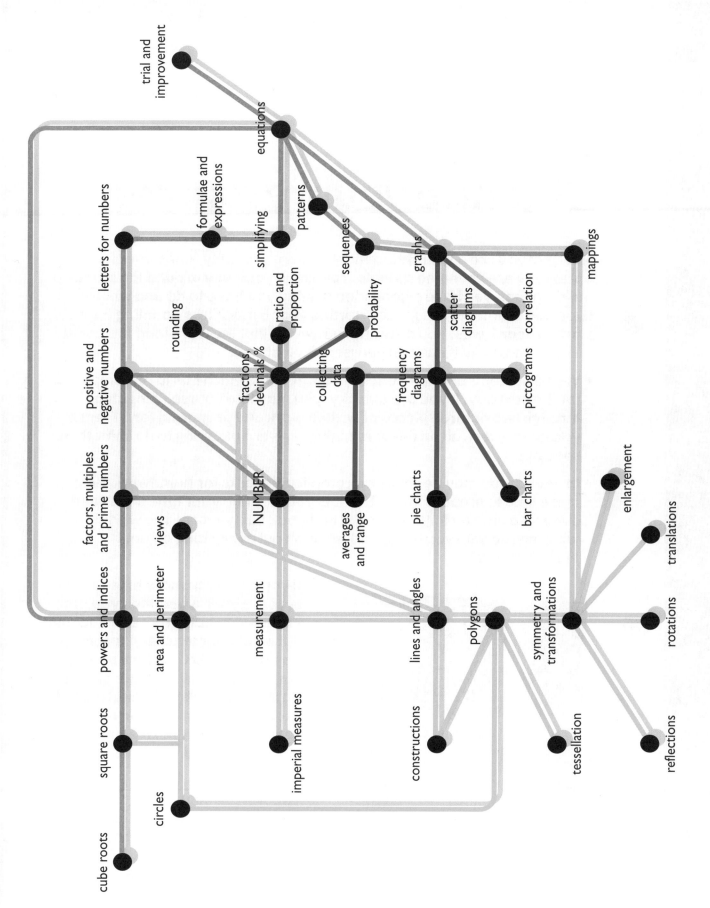

1

Organise your resources

Now that you are a year 8 student, you have probably found your feet, unless you are changing schools. You know your way around the school buildings and you have a good idea of what you have to do and what is expected of you. All this makes starting year 8 much less daunting than starting year 7 was. You may find, however, that the work load increases this year, so make it easy on yourself! Plan ahead.

- Year 8 students are quite often set homework which has to be completed for the next day. If you are unlucky, you may find yourself ploughing through two or three pieces of written work and preparing for a French vocabulary test, all on the very night you were planning to do something special.

- In year 8, you may be set more complicated tasks for homework, with more time to prepare them. This lets you arrange your time better and even take time off for that special night out, but beware! The work will catch up with you in the end, so don't put everything off until the last minute.

- If you are given more time to prepare your work, then you are expected to put in more. Try to find out what your teacher expects. You don't need to write a book, if your teacher just had four sides of A4 in mind! Make a careful note of exactly what you have to do and keep it somewhere safe until you have completed the task.

- You will probably need to research your subject. You could use books, other people or the Internet. Wherever you find the information, it's a pity to lose it.

6

- Keep all your notes together in a file or folder. Loose leaf files are useful as you can rearrange material when necessary.

- When you do find a good source of information, make a note of where you found it – the book, the website, the neighbour who so luckily turned out to know so much, the museum or library. You may need to go back and search for more information, and keeping notes will save you a lot of time.

- Use cheap, transparent, punched plastic pockets in A4 files to keep everything clean – it may save you having to write your work out again because it got dirty, crumpled or slept on by the cat. Different coloured files for different subjects can save time and cut out that frantic last minute search for the vital – and missing! – sheet of paper.

- If you are printing material from a computer, you can also try using different coloured paper or inks to help to keep things separate although it's usually better to hand in the finished piece on white paper and not a rainbow mix of colours.

Types of number

Understanding the jargon

An integer is a whole number. It can be positive, negative or zero.
A digit is an individual numeral in a number. 6 has one digit, 20 has two digits, as does 3.4.
A factor is a number which divides into another number without leaving a remainder.
A multiple is a number into which a factor will divide.
The product of two numbers is the result of multiplying them together.
The sum of two numbers is the result of adding them together.

Example
The product of two numbers is 50.
One of the numbers is 10. What is the other number?
$10 \times ? = 50$, so the missing number is $50 \div 10 = 5$.
Check your answer.
$10 \times 5 = 50$

Example
The sum of two numbers is 40.
One of the numbers is 15.
What is the other number?
$15 + ? = 40$, so the missing number is $40 - 15 = 25$.
Check your answer.
$15 + 25 = 40$.

Prime numbers

A prime number has two and only two factors – itself and 1.
1 has only one factor, so it is not a prime number.

Examples
17 is a prime number, because its only factors are 1 and 17.
23 is a prime number because its only factors are 1 and 23.

Exercise 1

1 The product of two numbers is 24.
   One of the numbers is 4.
   What is the other number?
2 The sum of two numbers is 30.
   One of the numbers is 17.
   What is the other number?

Tactics
3 is a *factor* of 12, or 2 is a factor of 10.
10 is a *multiple* of 5, or 21 is a multiple of 7.
The *product* of 5 and 2 is 10.
The *sum* of 5 and 2 is 7.

RED ALERT!   Calculators are not all the same. Read the instructions and practise using yours to work out squares and cubes, square roots and cube roots.   RED

Powers or indices

A number multiplied by itself produces a square number.
To find the square of a number on a calculator, use the x^2 button.
A number multiplied by itself and then multiplied by itself again produces a cube number.

Examples

- 25 is a square number because $5 \times 5 = 25$
  We can also write 25 as 5^2, read as 'five squared'.
- 1 is also a square number, because 1×1 or $1^2 = 1$
- $4^2 \times 4 = 4 \times 4 \times 4 = 4^3$ or 'four cubed'.
- $2 \times 2 \times 2 = 2^3 = 8$ 'two cubed is eight'.

A number multiplied by itself a number of times is raised to the power of that number.

Examples

- $2^4 = 2 \times 2 \times 2 \times 2 = 16$
  Two to the power of four is sixteen.
- $3^4 = 3 \times 3 \times 3 \times 3 = 81$
- $2^5 = 2 \times 2 \times 2 \times 2 \times 2 = 32$
  Two to the power of five is thirty-two.
- $3^5 = 3 \times 3 \times 3 \times 3 \times 3 = 243$

The small digits are powers or indices (singular is index).
To use a calculator to find 2^5 press 2 x^y 5 = or 2 y^x 5 =
In either case your calculator should display the answer 32.

Roots

A square root is the number which you multiply by itself to get a square number.
$5 \times 5 = 25$, so the square root of 25 is 5. $\sqrt{25} = 5$.
To find the square root of a number on a calculator, use the $\sqrt{}$ button.
A cube root is the number which you multiply by itself twice over to get a cubed number.
$2 \times 2 \times 2$ or $2^3 = 8$, so the cube root of 8 = 2.
The cube root sign is like the square root with a small 3 outside it like this: $\sqrt[3]{}$.

Examples

- $\sqrt{25} = 5$ because $5 \times 5 = 5^2 = 25$
- $\sqrt[3]{125} = 5$ because $5 \times 5 \times 5 = 5^3 = 125$
- $\sqrt{64} = 8$ because $8 \times 8 = 8^2 = 64$
- $\sqrt[3]{64} = 4$ because $4 \times 4 \times 4 = 4^3 = 64$

Exercise 2

1 $3^4 =$
2 $5^8 =$

Tactics

There is a quick and easy way to work out powers using a special key on the calculator.
On some calculators the button is marked x^y and on others it is y^x.

9

RED ALERT Remember 2^3 is not the same as 2×3.
$2^3 = 2 \times 2 \times 2 = 8$, whereas $2 \times 3 = 6$.
RED ALERT RED ALERT

Factors and multiples

Understanding the jargon

A prime factor of a number is a factor that is a prime number.
The highest common factor (HCF) is the largest number that will divide into two or more numbers without leaving a remainder.

Prime factors

> ### Example
> 2, 3, 4 and 6 are all factors of 12. 2 and 3 are prime numbers, so 2 and 3 are prime factors of 12. 6 is not a prime number, because 6 has the factors 1, 2, 3, 6.

How to write a number as a product of prime factors

> ### Example
> Write 120 as a product of prime factors. Unless you have a method you prefer, use a factor tree. Split 120 into a pair of factors with product 120. Continue to split each pair in the same way.
>
>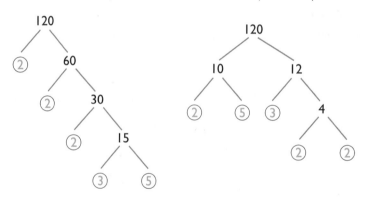
>
> When you reach a prime number at the end of the line, put a ring round it.
> When every line ends with a ringed prime number, you cannot go any further.
> $120 = 2 \times 2 \times 2 \times 3 \times 5$. This can be written with indices. $120 = 2^3 \times 3 \times 5$

Exercise 1

Write each number as a product of prime factors.

1 36
2 48
3 75
4 180

Tactics

There may be more than one way of developing the factor tree, but whichever route you choose, you should finish with the same numbers at the bottom.

Remember that one itself is not a prime number, so no line should end with a one.

How to find the highest common factor (HCF) of two numbers

Example

Find the HCF of 80 and 120.

First write 80 and 120 as products of prime factors.

(Try to work them out for yourself before looking at the answer.)

$80 = 2^4 \times 5$

$120 = 2^3 \times 3 \times 5$

Write one number under the other as a product of prime factors, in full, without indices.

$$80 = 2 \times 2 \times 2 \times 2 \qquad \times 5$$
$$120 = 2 \times 2 \times 2 \qquad \times 3 \times 5$$

Ring the numbers in pairs. Every time you have a pair, write the number down.

$$80 = 2 \times 2 \times 2 \times 2 \qquad \times 5$$
$$120 = 2 \times 2 \times 2 \qquad \times 3 \times 5$$

$2 \times 2 \times 2 \times 5 = 40$

The HCF of 80 and 120 is 40.

Example

Find the HCF of 150 and 360.

Write the factors and join up the pairs as before.

$$150 = 2 \qquad \times 3 \qquad \times 5 \times 5$$
$$360 = 2 \times 2 \times 2 \times 3 \times 3 \times 5$$

$2 \times 3 \times 5 = 30$

The HCF of 150 and 360 is 30.

If you have to list all the factors of a number, remember to include one and the number itself.

The factors of 60 are, 1, 2, 3, 4, 5, 6, 12, 15, 20, 30, 60.

Exercise 2

Find the highest common factor of each pair of numbers.

1   40 and 100

2   27 and 63

Tactics

When finding the HCF, start by splitting all the numbers into products of prime factors.

11

How to find the lowest common multiple (LCM)

When working with fractions, the lowest common denominator of the denominators is called the LCM.

Example
Find the LCM of 80 and 120.
Look again at the example on page 11, showing the HCF of 80 and 120.
You will see that the numbers without partners are an extra 2 and a 3.
Multiply the HCF by these extra, unmatched numbers.
$40 \times 2 \times 3 = 240$
The LCM of 80 and 120 is 240.

Example
Find the LCM of 45 and 60.

$$45 = 3 \times 3 \times 5$$
$$60 = 2 \times 2 \times 3 \times 5$$

$$②\times②\times③ \quad ③\times③\times⑤ \quad \times⑤$$

Those with partners are ③ and ⑤, and those without partners are ②, ② and ③.
The LCM is $3 \times 5 \times 2 \times 2 \times 3 = 180$
The LCM of 45 and 60 = 180.

A common multiple is any number into which two or more numbers will divide.
8, 16, 32, 64 etc are common multiples of 2, 4 and 8; but 8 is the lowest common multiple.

Exercise 3

Find the lowest common multiple of each pair of numbers.
1 30 and 45
2 12 and 16
3 4, 5 and 6

Tactics

It is very easy to find the lowest common multiple if you use the highest common factor as a starting point.

RED ALERT!   **The lowest common denominator is just the lowest common multiple of the denominators.**   RED

How to find the HCF or LCM of more than two numbers

Sometimes you may be asked to find the HCF or LCM of more than two numbers.
The method is almost the same.

Example

Find the LCM of 4, 6 and 8.

$4 = 2 \times 2$ There is a 2 in each line. Join them up and write down 2.

$6 = 2 \times 3$ There is a 2 in the first and third lines. Join them up and write another 2.

$8 = 2 \times 2 \times 2$ There is no 2 to join with the remaining 2, so put a ring round it.

There was no number left over for the 3, so put a ring round it.
Now multiply the list of factors, remembering to include the numbers which you have ringed.
$LCM = 2 \times 2 \times 2 \times 3 = 24$
The LCM of 4, 6 and 8 is 24.

Sometimes LCM and HCF calculations are wrapped up in words and are not obvious.

Example

Maria, William and David all visit the library. Maria goes every ten days, William every four days and David every twelve days. How often do their visits coincide?

$$
\left.
\begin{array}{l}
10 = \enclose{circle}{2} \qquad \times \enclose{circle}{5} \\
4 = \enclose{circle}{2} \times \enclose{circle}{2} \\
12 = \enclose{circle}{2} \times \enclose{circle}{2} \times \enclose{circle}{3}
\end{array}
\right\} \quad 2 \times 2 \times 3 \times 5 = 60
$$

There is a 2 in each line.
This is the HCF.
Multiply the HCF by all the unmatched factors to find the LCM.
Their visits will coincide every sixty days.

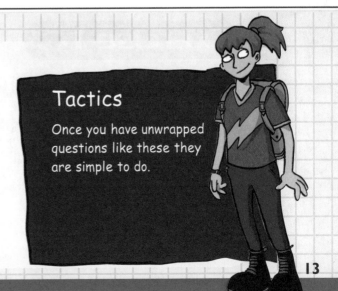

Exercise 4

A number 157 bus leaves the garage every eight minutes, a number 93 leaves the garage every ten minutes and a number 192 every twelve minutes. A 157, a 93 and a 192 all leave together at 10.00 a.m. When is the next time that a 157, a 93 and a 192 are due to leave at the same time?

Tactics

Once you have unwrapped questions like these they are simple to do.

ERT   **Make sure you know the difference between the HCF and LCM – the terms can be confusing.**   RED ALERT

Fractions, decimals and percentages

How to change decimals to fractions

Whole numbers	.	tenths	hundredths	thousandths	ten thousandths
3	.	0	I		
3	.	0	0	I	
3	.	0	0	0	I

Here is the easy way to do this:
*   Write the whole number.
*   Write the decimal part of the number as a numerator, starting with the first non-zero digit after the point.
*   For the denominator, write a 1 instead of the point and a 0 under each of the decimal places after the point.
Cancel if necessary.

> Examples
> $\cdot\ 0.9 = \frac{9}{10}$ $\cdot\ 0.09 = \frac{9}{100}$ $\cdot\ 0.4 = \frac{4}{10} = \frac{2}{5}$

How to change decimals to percentages

Round the number to two decimal places (2 d.p.).
Multiply the result by 100 and write the answer as a percentage.

> Examples
> $\cdot\ 0.34 = 34\%$
> $\cdot\ 0.467 = 0.47$ (2 d.p.) $= 47\%$

Exercise 1

Fill in the gaps.

1   $0.5 = \frac{\square}{10} = \frac{\square}{\square}$

2   $0.8 = \frac{\square}{10} = \frac{\square}{\square}$

3   $0.75 = \frac{\square}{100} = \frac{\square}{\square} = \frac{\square}{\square}$

4   $0.32 = \frac{\square}{100} = \frac{\square}{\square}$

Tactics

There is a reminder about cancelling on page 16.

Remember, 0.6 = 60% and 0.06 = 6%

How to change fractions to decimals

Just divide the numerator by the denominator.

numerator
denominator

> **Example**
>
> Write $\frac{3}{8}$ as a decimal.
>
> $3 \div 8 = 0.375$

Sometimes the answer goes on for ever.

$\frac{1}{3} = 1 \div 3 = 0.3333\ldots$

This is a recurring or repeating decimal.

It is written with a dot over the 3 as $0.\dot{3}$.

If the repeating pattern has more than one digit, write the number with dots over the first and last digit, or draw a line over them.

> **Example**
>
> 0.171 717 is written as $0.\dot{1}\dot{7}$ or $0.\overline{17}$.

Some decimals go on for ever, but without any pattern.
You will learn more about these next year.

Exercise 2

Fill in the gaps.

1 $\frac{3}{4} = 0.$_____ = _____%

2 _____ = $\frac{2}{10}$ = 0.2 = 20%

Tactics

Some recurring decimals have very large groups of digits. Try working out $\frac{1}{13}$, $\frac{1}{17}$ or $\frac{1}{19}$ – you will have to do it without a calculator!

ERT

**Recurring decimals can always be changed to fractions.
This is not true for all decimals.**

RED ALERT

Working with fractions

Understanding the jargon

An integer is a whole number. It can be positive or negative (such as $-3, -16$). Zero is also an integer.
A mixed number is a whole number, or integer, plus a fraction ($1\frac{1}{4}, 3\frac{1}{5}, 5\frac{2}{3}$).
An improper fraction is a fraction with the numerator bigger than the denominator ($\frac{5}{4}, \frac{16}{5}, \frac{17}{3}$).
A mixed number can be written as an improper fraction.
Improper fractions are also called top-heavy fractions.

Equivalent fractions

Two or more fractions that are worth the same are equivalent fractions.
One-half and two-quarters are equivalent fractions.
To make equivalent fractions for a given fraction, multiply (or divide) the numerator and the denominator by the same number.

Cancelling – reducing to lowest terms

This means finding fractions that are equivalent to a given fraction, by dividing both top and bottom by the same number.

Reciprocal

Find the reciprocal of a number by turning it upside down.
The reciprocal of $\frac{2}{5}$ is $\frac{5}{2}$.
$10 = \frac{10}{1}$ so the reciprocal of 10 is $\frac{1}{10}$.

Exercise 1

Cancel these fractions to their lowest terms.

1 $\frac{15}{20}$ **2** $\frac{18}{72}$ **3** $\frac{15}{90}$

4 $\frac{28}{64}$ **5** $\frac{37}{111}$ **6** $\frac{72}{360}$

Tactics

Fractions are in their lowest terms when there are no more common factors to cancel.

RED ALERT! The fractions will only be equivalent if you multiply (or divide) the numerator and the denominator by the *same* number.

Adding fractions

$\frac{1}{2} + \frac{1}{4} = \frac{3}{4}$

Change the half to two quarters, and then add the remaining quarter.

This gives the clue for adding any fractions together. If the fractions are from different families, one or both must be changed, so that they all have the same denominator. This is called finding a common denominator and is similar to finding the lowest common multiple.

Example

$\frac{1}{3} + \frac{1}{5}$ The lowest common multiple of 3 and 5 is 15.

$\frac{1}{3} + \frac{1}{5} = \frac{5}{15} + \frac{3}{15} = \frac{8}{15}$

If your calculation involves whole numbers, add them together separately.

$4\frac{1}{5} + 2\frac{1}{3} = 4\frac{3}{15} + 2\frac{5}{15}$

$\qquad\qquad = 6\frac{8}{15}$

Examples

Find the lowest common denominators (LCM of the denominators) of these sets of fractions.

- $\frac{\square}{15} \quad \frac{\square}{5} \quad \frac{\square}{10} \quad \frac{\square}{30}$ LCM of 5, 10, 15 and 30 is 30.

- $\frac{\square}{2} \quad \frac{\square}{6} \quad \frac{\square}{12} \quad \frac{\square}{3}$ LCM of 2, 3, 6 and 12 is 12.

Examples

- $\frac{1}{2} + \frac{1}{8} = \frac{4}{8} + \frac{1}{8} = \frac{5}{8}$ • $1\frac{1}{3} + 1\frac{1}{10} = 1\frac{10}{30} + 1\frac{3}{30}$ • $4\frac{1}{5} + 3\frac{1}{10} = 4\frac{2}{10} + 3\frac{1}{10}$

$\qquad\qquad\qquad\qquad\qquad\qquad\qquad\qquad = 2\frac{13}{30} \qquad\qquad\qquad\qquad = 7\frac{3}{10}$

Exercise 2

Work these out

1   $6\frac{1}{4} + 2\frac{1}{10}$

2   $5\frac{1}{16} + 1\frac{1}{4}$

Tactics

Always check your answer at the end to make sure that you have given it in its lowest terms.

Subtracting fractions

Example

$5\frac{9}{16} - 3\frac{7}{16} = 2\frac{2}{16} = 2\frac{1}{8}$

Sometimes the fractional part of the second number is larger than the fractional part of the first.

Example

$5\frac{3}{16} - 3\frac{7}{16}$

There are several methods of tackling this, but here is an easy way.

Think of the 5 as 4 + 1. Keep the 4 intact, change the 1 into $\frac{16}{16}$ making $4 + \frac{16}{16}$.

Adding the original $\frac{3}{16}$ makes $4 + \frac{16}{16} + \frac{3}{16} = 4 + \frac{19}{16}$

The original calculation becomes $4\frac{19}{16} - 3\frac{7}{16} = 1\frac{12}{16} = 1\frac{3}{4}$

Example

$7\frac{1}{3} - 2\frac{7}{8}$ 　　　　　Start by finding the lowest common denominator.

$\frac{1}{3} = \frac{8}{24}$ 　　$\frac{7}{8} = \frac{21}{24}$ 　　The lowest common denominator is 24.

So $7\frac{1}{3} - 2\frac{7}{8} = 7\frac{8}{24} - 2\frac{21}{24}$ 　　$7\frac{1}{3} = 7\frac{8}{24} = 7 + \frac{8}{24}$ and $7 = 6 + \frac{24}{24}$ so $7\frac{1}{3} = 6 + \frac{24}{24} + \frac{8}{24} = 6\frac{32}{24}$

$7\frac{1}{3} - 2\frac{7}{8} = 6\frac{32}{24} - 2\frac{21}{24} = 4\frac{11}{24}$

Exercise 3

Give the answers in their lowest terms.

1　$6\frac{2}{3} - 3\frac{11}{12}$

2　$4\frac{3}{8} - 2\frac{1}{10}$

Tactics

Knowing your multiplication tables helps with cancelling.

18

Cancelling often makes the calculation easier, but _each time_ you cancel, you _must_ cancel one number from the numerator and one from the denominator.

Multiplying fractions

Multiplying fractions is easy! Multiply the numerators together and multiply the denominators together. In other words, multiply along the top and multiply along the bottom.

The importance of cancelling

Example

$\frac{5}{8} \times \frac{4}{15}$

$\frac{5 \times 4}{8 \times 15} = \frac{20}{120} = \frac{1}{6}$

This calculation can be made even easier by cancelling.

$5 \times 4 = 4 \times 5$, so $\frac{5 \times 4}{8 \times 15} = \frac{4 \times 5}{8 \times 15}$

Splitting the calculation gives $\frac{4}{8} \times \frac{5}{15}$

But $\frac{4}{8} = \frac{1}{2}$ and $\frac{5}{15} = \frac{1}{3}$ so $\frac{4}{8} \times \frac{5}{15} = \frac{1}{2} \times \frac{1}{3} = \frac{1 \times 1}{2 \times 3} = \frac{1}{6}$

Examples

- $\frac{3}{5} \times \frac{7}{12} = \frac{1}{5} \times \frac{7}{4} = \frac{7}{20}$
- $\frac{4}{7} \times \frac{3}{8} = \frac{1}{7} \times \frac{3}{2} = \frac{3}{14}$

You can cancel even if one number isn't directly on top of the other.

How to multiply mixed numbers

Example

$2\frac{1}{2} \times 1\frac{1}{2}$

Half of $2\frac{1}{2} = 1\frac{1}{4}$ $1 \times 2\frac{1}{2} = 2\frac{1}{2}$ The total is $1\frac{1}{4} + 2\frac{1}{2} = 3\frac{3}{4}$

Although it might seem logical to work out 2×1 and $\frac{1}{2} \times \frac{1}{2}$, this would give the answer $2\frac{1}{4}$, which is wrong.

Whenever you multiply mixed numbers, remember to change them first into improper fractions. Then cancel and multiply as usual.

$\frac{5}{2} \times \frac{3}{2} = \frac{15}{4} = 3\frac{3}{4}$

Exercise 4

1 $\frac{2}{5} \times \frac{15}{22}$

2 $\frac{3}{4} \times \frac{5}{8}$

Tactics

Cancelling is sometimes called 'reducing to lowest terms'.

Exercise 5

Give the answers in their lowest terms.

1 $2\frac{3}{4} \times 1\frac{1}{8}$ 2 $6\frac{3}{4} \times 2\frac{2}{9}$

RED ALERT Always check that the final answer is in its lowest terms and is not a improper fraction. RED ALERT RED ALERT

How to divide fractions

When trying to understand how to divide fractions, it is easier if you look at division in the following way.

Examples

- $10 \div 2$ This is really asking,

  'How many twos make ten?' $10 \div 2 = 5$

- $10 \div \frac{1}{2}$ How many halves in ten?

  $10 \div \frac{1}{2} = 20.$

  In other words, $10 \times 2 = 20$

- $3 \div \frac{1}{4}$ How many quarters make 3?

  $3 \div \frac{1}{4} = 12.$

  In other words, $3 \times 4 = 12$

Example

$6 \div \frac{3}{4}$

Start by finding the number of separate quarters in six. $6 \times 4 = 24$

The question asks for them to be in groups of 3. $24 \div 3 = 8$

$\frac{6}{1} \div \frac{3}{4} = \frac{6}{1} \times \frac{4}{3}$

Example

$10 \div \frac{2}{5}$

Splitting ten into fifths gives fifty separate pieces. $10 \times 5 = 50$

But they are to be in groups of 2. $50 \div 2 = 25$

$\frac{10}{1} \div \frac{2}{5} = \frac{10}{1} \times \frac{5}{2} = \frac{50}{2} = 25$

To divide one fraction by another, multiply the first fraction by the second number turned upside down, i.e. by its reciprocal.

Example

$\frac{3}{7} \div \frac{15}{28} = \frac{3}{7} \times \frac{28}{15} = \frac{1}{7} \times \frac{28}{5} = \frac{1}{1} \times \frac{4}{5} =$

Example

$\frac{5}{16} \div \frac{3}{8}$

$\frac{5}{16} \div \frac{3}{8} = \frac{5}{16} \times \frac{8}{3} = \frac{5}{2} \times \frac{1}{3} = \frac{5}{6}$

Exercise 6

1 $\frac{9}{44} \div \frac{6}{11}$

2 $\frac{2}{5} \div \frac{12}{25}$

Tactics

You should still get the right answer if you left the cancelling to the end, however, it's usually better to cancel early on to avoid hefty calculations.

RED ALERT! **You must invert the fraction, i.e. turn it upside down, before you cancel.**

How to divide mixed numbers

Always change the mixed numbers into improper or top-heavy fractions.
Turn the second fraction upside down (i.e. find its reciprocal) and proceed as for multiplication.

> ### Examples
>
> a $\quad 4\frac{3}{8} \div 1\frac{5}{16} = \frac{35}{8} \div \frac{21}{16} = \frac{35}{8} \times \frac{16}{21} = \frac{5}{1} \times \frac{2}{3} = \frac{10}{3} = 3\frac{1}{3}$
>
> b $\quad 4\frac{2}{5} \div 3\frac{3}{5} = \frac{22}{5} \div \frac{18}{5} = \frac{22}{5} \times \frac{5}{18} = \frac{11}{1} \times \frac{1}{9} = \frac{11}{9} = 1\frac{2}{9}$

How to use your calculator with fractions

Most calculators have a key that looks something like this. $\boxed{a^{b}/c}$
To key in a fraction, e.g. $4\frac{1}{2}$, press $\boxed{4}$ $\boxed{a^{b}/c}$ $\boxed{1}$ $\boxed{a^{b}/c}$ $\boxed{2}$. The calculator will perform whatever instruction you give it, and will give the answer as a fraction in its lowest terms.
If you have to change an improper fraction to a mixed number, key in the fraction as usual, and then press $\boxed{=}$. The calculator will automatically convert it.
A calculator will give any fraction in its lowest terms. This is often useful in probability questions where you have a fraction involving very large numbers. Key it in to the calculator and press $\boxed{=}$.

How to use a calculator to change a fraction to a decimal

Key in the fraction or carry out the calculation in the usual way, then press $\boxed{=}$.
Press the fraction key again and the fraction will turn into a decimal.
Your calculator will also be able to turn a mixed number into an improper fraction, though this may involve using the $\boxed{SHIFT}$ or $\boxed{INV}$ key.
Some – but not all – calculators will turn decimals into fractions.
Models and makes of calculator vary in what they will and will not do. Experiment with yours, or, better still, read the instructions and find out how yours can help you.

Exercise 7

Give the answers in their lowest terms.

1 $\quad 6\frac{1}{4} \div 3\frac{1}{8}$

2 $\quad 5\frac{1}{7} \div 1\frac{1}{8}$

Tactics

Remember: A scientific calculator always carries out operations in the following order:
B Brackets
o Powers or roots
D Divide
M Multiply
A Add
S Subtract

21

Fractions in a nutshell

Adding fractions...
1 Add the whole numbers together.
2 Change the denominators where necessary so that all fractions have a common denominator.
3 Add the numerators.
4 If the answer is an improper fraction, convert it to a mixed number and cancel if necessary to make sure that the answer is in its lowest terms.

...subtracting fractions
1 Make sure both fractions have the same (common) denominator.
2 If first number includes a smaller fraction than the second number does, change one of its whole numbers into a fraction with the same denominator, to make an improper fraction.
3 Subtract the whole numbers and the fractions.
4 Cancel if necessary so that the answer is in its lowest terms.

Multiplying fractions...
1 Change any mixed numbers to improper fractions.
2 Cancel where possible.
3 Multiply the numerators together and the denominators together.
4 If the answer is an improper fraction, change it back to a mixed number, and check that the final answer is in its lowest terms.

...dividing fractions
1 Change any mixed numbers into improper fractions.
2 Change the division sign to a multiplication sign and turn the second fraction upside down (i.e. its reciprocal).
3 Cancel if possible, then multiply the numerators together and the denominators together.
4 Change the answer back to a mixed number if necessary, and make sure that it is in its lowest terms.

Exercise 8

1 $3\frac{2}{5} + 1\frac{2}{3}$

2 $5\frac{1}{4} - 2\frac{3}{8}$

3 $2\frac{3}{16} \times 1\frac{5}{7}$

4 $6\frac{3}{4} \div 2\frac{1}{2}$

Tactics
If you are going to use your calculator for fractions, make sure you know how to do it.

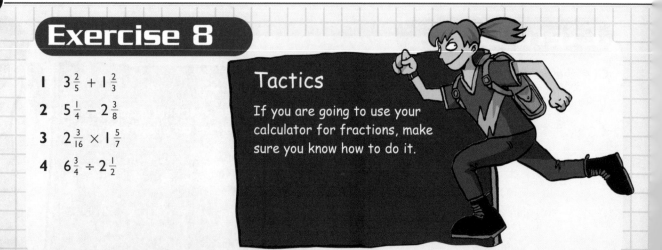

2

Organise those fractions

You will find that fractions, particularly adding and multiplying, keep cropping up in maths. Obvious examples are in area and volume questions. You will also need to add and multiply fractions, though without whole numbers, to solve probability questions for GCSE. Fractions are easy if you are allowed to use a calculator, but you will need a good basic understanding if there is a question involving fractions on a non–calculator paper.

If you find fractions really difficult, concentrate on:
- cancelling or reducing fractions to their lowest terms
- switching between fractions, decimals and percentages
- adding simple fractions with the same or different denominators but without whole numbers
- subtracting a simple fraction, without a whole number, from 1
- multiplying fractions, but without whole numbers

Multiplying and dividing decimals

How to multiply by a decimal

The actual multiplying process is exactly the same as it is for any form of multiplication, but you do have to be careful to put the decimal point in the right position.

Example

• 0.1×0.3

This is easier to understand, when you remember than $0.1 = \frac{1}{10}$ and $0.3 = \frac{3}{10}$.

$\frac{1}{10} \times \frac{3}{10} = \frac{3}{100}$

But $\frac{3}{100} = 0.03$, so $0.1 \times 0.3 = 0.03$

• 2.34×0.3

Firstly, work out the calculation as if there were no decimal points.

$$234$$
$$\times \ 3$$
$$\overline{702}$$

$0.34 = \frac{3}{100}$ and $0.3 = \frac{3}{10}$

$\frac{?}{100} \times \frac{?}{10} = \frac{?}{1000}$

This means that the answer must be in thousandths.

As the question has three decimals places, the answer must have three decimal places.

$2.34 \times 0.3 = 0.702$

Multiplying decimals in a nutshell

1   Work out the calculation as if you were multiplying whole numbers.
2   Count the number of digits after the decimal points in both numbers in the question.
3   Put a decimal point in the answer to give the same number of digits after the point.

Exercise 1

1   0.4×0.6
2   0.03×1.7

Tactics

The divisor is the number by which you are dividing. In $6 \div 2$ the divisor is 2.

RED ALERT **To make sure that you get the decimal point in the right place in the answer, the *divisor* has to be a whole number.** RE

Dividing decimals...

...by a whole number
This is very easy as it is just like any other form of division.

$8.4 \div 2 = 4.2$

$1.2 \div 4 = 0.3$

...by a decimal
This may be easier to understand if you look back to fractions.

$6 \div \frac{1}{2} = 12$, so $6 \div 0.5$ has to come to 12.

The easiest way is to turn the divisor (number by which you are dividing) into a whole number, in this case by multiplying it by 10 to make it 5. However, to get the right answer, you need to multiply both numbers by the same amount. $60 \div 5 = 12$.

If this seems a strange idea, try some examples without decimals.

$8 \div 2 = 4$

$80 \div 20 = ?$

$800 \div 200 = ?$

Examples

- $7.2 \div 0.2$ Multiplying both numbers by 10 gives $72 \div 2 = 36$.
- $5.4 \div 0.02$ This time you need to multiply by 100.

$5.4 \div 0.02 = 540 \div 2 = 270$

- $3.468 \div 0.2 = 34.68 \div 2 = 17.34$

Dividing decimals in a nutshell

1   The divisor (i.e. the number by which you are dividing) must be a whole number.
   If necessary, 'move' the decimal point the required number of places to the right.
2   'Move' the decimal point of the other number the same number of places.
   Add noughts to the end of the number if necessary.
3   Divide one number by the other as usual.

Exercise 2

Do not use a calculator for this exercise.

1 $0.4 \div 0.2$

2 $3.6 \div 0.03$

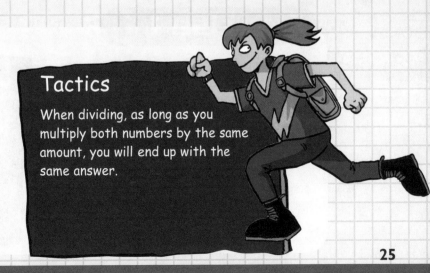

Tactics

When dividing, as long as you multiply both numbers by the same amount, you will end up with the same answer.

ERT   **The decimal point doesn't actually move.**
The digits do – but it is easier to think of it this way.   RED ALERT

Percentages

Easy percentages

1% = one hundredth or 0.01

10% = one tenth or 0.1

20% = 2 × 10%

5% = $\frac{1}{2}$ of 10%

15% = 10% + 5%

25% = $\frac{1}{4}$

12.5% or 12$\frac{1}{2}$% = $\frac{1}{2}$ of 25%

50% = $\frac{1}{2}$

75% = $\frac{3}{4}$

How to turn a decimal into a percentage

1 Write the decimal to two decimal places.
2 Multiply the result by 100.

Examples
0.75 = 75%
0.621 = 0.62 (2 d.p.) = 62%
0.148 = 0.15 (2 d.p.) = 15%
0.09 = 9%
0.4 = 0.40 = 40%

How to turn a fraction into a percentage

1 Change the fraction to a decimal by dividing the numerator by the denominator.
2 Multiply the decimal by 100.

Example

Change $\frac{3}{5}$ to a percentage.

$\frac{3}{5} \times 100 = 3 \times 20 = 60\%$ (Cancel the 5 and

the 100 before you start.)

Example

In a class of 25 pupils, 5 wore glasses.

What percentage wore glasses?

5 pupils out of 25 = $\frac{5}{25}$

$\frac{5}{25} \times 100 = 20\%$

Exercise 1

1 Change these decimals to percentages.
   a 0.5   b 0.25   c 0.45   d 1.5
2 Change these fractions into percentages.
   a $\frac{3}{4}$ b $\frac{3}{8}$ c $\frac{9}{10}$ d $\frac{7}{20}$ e $\frac{55}{88}$

Tactics

You can often make a percentage that you don't know by using the ones that you do.
e.g. 35% = 20% + 15%

RED ALERT!

Remember, per cent means 'out of a hundred'.
The whole, original amount is 100%.

RED

Example

Helen scored 16 out of 20 in a maths test. What percentage was that?

16 out of 20 is usually written as $\frac{16}{20}$. Change this to a percentage in the usual way.

$\frac{16}{20} \times 100 = 16 \times 5 = 80\%$

How to find a percentage of a number

Examples

- Find 16% of £56.25.

  Using decimals:

  $1\% = 0.01$

  1% of £56.25 = £56.25 $\times$ 0.01

  $\qquad\qquad\qquad = £0.5625$

  $16\% = £0.5625 \times 16$

  $\qquad\quad = £9.00$

- Find 16% of £272.00.

  Using fractions:

  $16\% = \frac{16}{100}$

  16% of £272.00 $= \frac{16}{100} \times 272$

  $\qquad\qquad\qquad\quad = £43.52$

Percentages in everyday life

Example

The price of a jacket costing £60.00 is reduced in a sale by 10%.

What is the sale price?

10% of £60.00 = £6.00

The reduced price is £60.00 – £6.00 = £54.00

Exercise 2

1 Find
   a 15% of £50   b 24% of £80
   c 45% of £120   d 72% of £350

2 The price of a washing machine is reduced by $12\frac{1}{2}\%$ in a sale. Its price before the sale was £320. Find
   a the reduction in the price
   b the sale price.

Tactics

If you can say, 'out of', write the amount as a fraction and multiply it by 100.

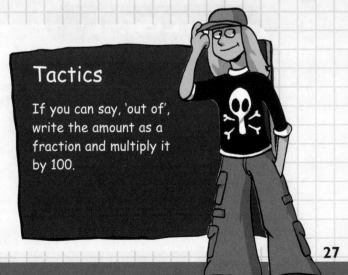

ERT RED ALERT RED ALERT! RED ALERT RED ALERT

Ratio

A ratio splits a group into parts, and compares the proportion of one part to another.
If there are 24 pupils in a class and 6 learn Spanish, the ratio of Spanish to non-Spanish learners is 6 : 18 or 1 : 3.
The ratio of non-Spanish to Spanish learners is 18 : 6 or 3 : 1.

How to work out a ratio

Example

Jane is mixing purple paint. She uses three tins of red paint and two tins of blue. The ratio of red tins to blue is 3 : 2.
If she wanted twice as much purple paint, she would use six tins of red and four of blue. 6 : 4 = 3 : 2

Be careful to double the quantities and not add two tins to each colour.

When you divide ratios until there are no common factors except one, it is called 'simplifying a ratio' or writing a ratio in its 'simplest form'.

100 : 50 = 2 : 1
3.5 : 10.5 = 1 : 3

Exercise 1

Reduce these ratios to their lowest terms.
1 12 : 9 = 4 : ☐
2 24 : 18 = 12 : ☐ = ☐ : 3
3 36 : 15 = 12 : ☐
4 48 : 27 = ☐ : ☐

Tactics

Ratios are rather like fractions. Always express them in their lowest forms.

Example

Lawrence has mixed brown paint using red, green and yellow in the ratio 3 : 2 : 1.

a   If he used four tins of green, how much red and yellow did he use?

b   How much brown paint did he use altogether?

Write the information like this.

R	:	G	:	Y
3		2		1
		4		

You can easily see that he has doubled the amount of green, so he will need to double the amount of red and yellow.

Example

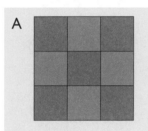

A

In this pattern, the fraction of orange squares is $\frac{5}{9}$.

The fraction of blue squares is $\frac{4}{9}$.

The ratio of orange to blue squares is 5 : 4.

Example

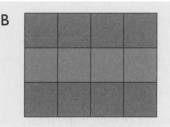

B

In this pattern, the fraction of blue squares is $\frac{4}{12} = \frac{1}{3}$.

The fraction of orange squares is $\frac{2}{3}$.

The ratio of orange to blue squares is 8 : 4 = 2 : 1.

If the pattern repeated, the ratio is always 2 : 1.

Exercise 2

This pattern represents a corner of a board on a stall at a school fair.

Contestants roll a counter on the board and win a prize if it lands on a plum.

C

1   In this pattern, the ratio of losing to winning squares is ___ : ___ .

2   The ratio of winning to losing squares is ___ : ___ .

3   What fraction of the board consists of winning squares?

4   The whole board contains 48 squares in an identical pattern. How many of them would not be winning squares?

Positive and negative numbers

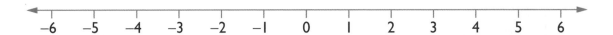

All numbers have a place somewhere on a never-ending number line.
When a number has a value of less than zero, it is a negative number.
So −3 is read as 'negative 3' and −1.5 is read as 'negative 1.5'.

How to add and subtract two negative numbers

$(+6) + (+2) = 6 + 2 = 8$ If two signs next to each other are the same, replace with a positive.

$(−6) − (−2) = −6 + 2 = −4$
$(−6) + (+2) = −6 + 2 = −4$ If two signs next to each other are different, replace with a negative.

$(+6) − (+2) = 6 − 2 = 4$
$(+6) + (−2) = 6 − 2 = 4$

Numbers like this are often called directed numbers.

Another way to work out adding and subtracting positive and negative numbers is to imagine a celsius thermometer. Numbers which fall below zero are negative or 'minus' numbers.

Exercise 1

1   $(−2) + (+8)$

2   $(+10) − (+6)$

3   $(−8) + (+8)$

4   $(−1) + (−8)$

Tactics

In the 'real world', for instance on a weather forecast, you will hear negative numbers referred to as 'minus numbers'. The forecaster may say, 'The temperature tonight will be minus eight.'

RED ALERT!   **This can be hard to remember.**
Same and poSitive each have the letter S.   ALERT REC

How to multiply and divide negative numbers

> **Example**
>
> Suppose you owe a friend £2.00. You will have £2.00 less or −2 pounds.
>
> Unfortunately for you, three other friends remember that you also owe each of them £2.00. You owe £8.00 altogether.
>
> $4 \times -2 = -8$
>
> However, your friends take pity on you and cancel the debt. You no longer owe four friends any money. You are eight pounds richer than you thought you would be.
>
> $-4 \times -2 = 8$

When multiplying or dividing two numbers:

* if two signs are the same, the answer will be positive
* if two signs are different, the answer will be negative.

> **Examples**
>
> * $3 \times -2 = -6$
> * $-4 \times 5 = -20$
> * $-4 \times -5 = 20$
> * $8 \times 4 = 32$

Be very careful not to mix up the rules for adding or subtracting with those for multiplying or dividing.

> **Examples**
>
> * $-6 -5 = -11$ * $3 + (-2) = 3 - 2 = 1$
> * $-6 \times -5 = 30$ * $3 \times -2 = -6$

Exercise 2

1. $6 \div 2$
2. $-16 \div -2$
3. $-10 \div 5$
4. $-20 \div 10$

Tactics

Remember, if there is no sign in front of it, the number is assumed to be positive: $3 = (+3)$.

3

Organise your learning

As you progress, you will find that the work load increases and there is more to learn. There are all sorts of ways of helping yourself. Before you get really bogged down, try out some of these ideas to see which ones work best for you.

- If possible, find a place which you can use regularly for work and will come to associate with studying. Even if it's a corner of a shared bedroom, see if there's room for a table or desk and a safe place for all your books and other equipment which by now you have probably collected. If it's not possible to work at home, you may have a local library or a school homework club you can use. Sometimes this is better than home, because of the extra resources conveniently to hand.

- Several short sessions of study are better than one long one. Most people find that their concentration wanders after an hour – sometimes less – so give yourself plenty of ten–minute breaks, but don't make the breaks too long as it's sometimes hard to motivate yourself to get back to work.

- During the break, do something completely different. Have a cup of tea or coffee, or whatever else you fancy, and perhaps something to eat. Best of all, when possible get some fresh air, even if it just means opening a window.

- Take a break just before you run out of ideas. Jot down a reminder if you're afraid of forgetting something vital. Knowing exactly what to do next makes restarting so much easier. Alternatively, you can make a fresh start with a fresh subject.

- Try to decide before you start what you hope to achieve in the session, This can save a lot of time and effort. Always be prepared to change or adapt your plan once you get going.

- If you have a task which involves reading through a fairly lengthy passage before you start, skim through quickly to get a rough general idea of what it's all about. Then go back and read it more carefully, making notes as you go.

- Try out different methods of taking notes and planning essays. Some people like to make notes in lists whilst others prefer a more visual, diagrammatic approach. Try using coloured pens, pencils or highlighters. This may make the information easier to remember and can certainly make it stand out, and thus easier to find again.

- Very few people can read something just once and remember it for ever. Don't worry if, like most of us, you're not one of the favoured few. Going over work at frequent intervals really does help you to learn, though. If you learn something for homework one night, try to go over it again the following morning. Don't panic if you seem to have lost it all. It's still buried there in the recesses of your brain. Keep going over it, and little by little it will stick.

- If possible, try to use what you have learned. This is particularly useful in a subject like maths as you will not know if you can do something until you try to work out an example. Keep your old exercise books and worksheets as they may hold clues on how to do things you could handle six months ago but have now forgotten.

- Try teaching a friend something that you think you can do. (If your friend was away from school the day you learned it, so much the better.) He or she will soon tell you if you know what you are talking about.

- If you are interested in a subject, try finding out more from people who know more about it than you do, from books, or from the Internet.

- Sometimes, reading the same information but put in a slightly different way can help you to remember it, and also increase your knowledge and understanding. Hopefully, you will find the subject interesting in its own right, but, even if not, it might come in useful in a piece of work at a later date so keep a note of what you have found, and where you found it. You never know. You might be lucky and next week's homework will be sitting there, done, just needing a few minutes' polishing.

Basics of algebra

Putting values in expressions

If $s = 10$ and $t = 5$

st means $s \times t$	$10 \times 5 = 50$
$\dfrac{s}{t}$ means $s \div t$	$10 \div 5 = 2$
$3s$ means $3 \times s$	$3 \times 10 = 30$
$s + s + s + s = 4s$	$10 + 10 + 10 + 10 = 4 \times 10 = 40$
s^2 means $s \times s$	$10 \times 10 = 100$
$(2s)^2$ means $2s \times 2s = 4s^2$	$20 \times 20 = 400$ or $4 \times 10 \times 10 = 400$
$2s^2$ means $2 \times s \times s$	$2 \times 10 \times 10 = 200$

How to work with formulae

> ### Example
> Jack is twelve years old. His sister is four years younger.
> His sister is $12 - 4 = 8$.

The way to find out his sister's age is to subtract 4 years from Jack's age.
Put into the language of algebra, if Jack is n years old, his sister is $n - 4$ years old.

> ### Example
> Paul is saving up for a bike.
> His parents say that they will give him the same amount of money that he manages to save.
> Paul saves p pounds, so with his parents' contribution he will have $2 \times p = 2p$ pounds.
> His aunt gives him another 5 pounds, so altogether he has $2p + 5$ pounds.
> If he saves £50.00, he has $2 \times 50 + 5 = £105$.
> If he saves £15.00, he has $2 \times 15 + 5 = £35.00$.

Exercise 1

If $a = 3$ and $b = 5$, work out the value
of each expression.

1 $a + b$
2 $3a - b$
3 $b - a$
4 $b^2 - a^2$

Tactics

A *formula* (plural, formulae) is
simply a set of instructions or
rules written algebraically.
Parts of formulae (on one side of
the $=$ sign) are called expressions.

**Make sure you know the difference
between $(2t)^2$ and $2t^2$.**

Shapes and expressions

These shapes are drawn on dotted squared paper using lines of length f and length g.
An expression for the perimeter of this rectangle is:
$f + f + f + f + f + f = 6f$

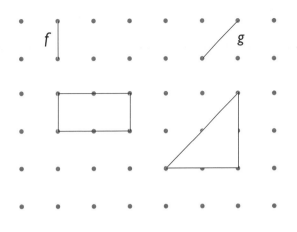

Example
Find an expression for the perimeter of the triangle.
$2f + 2f + 2g = 4f + 2g$

Simplifying expressions

Examples
- $r + r + r = 3r$
- $r + 3 + r + 6 = r + r + 3 + 6 = 2r + 9$
- $3r + r = 4r$

- $5r - 2r = 3r$
- $6r + r + r^2 = 7r + r^2$

Example
Penny made a pile of two bags of red discs and five bags of blue discs.
There were r red discs in each bag of red discs and b blue discs in each bag of blue discs.
Altogether there were $2r + 5b$ discs.
Jenny made another pile, so there were two identical piles.
Altogether there were $2 \times (2r + 5b)$ or $(2r + 5b) \times 2$ or $2(2r + 5b)$ discs.

Exercise 2

1. Write an expression for the perimeter of each of these shapes. Write each expression in its simplest form.
2. Simplify these expressions.
   a. $r + s + r + s + r + s$
   b. $4a + 3b + 2a - 3b$
   c. $x + y + 2xy + 3yx$
   d. $p + p^2 + 2pq + 4p - pq$

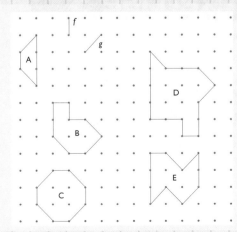

Do not mix up r^2 and $2r$. If $r = 3$, $r^2 = 9$ and $2r = 6$.
Be careful. $(r + b) \times 2$ is not the same as $r + b \times 2$.
Remember, in maths always multiply or divide before adding or subtracting.

ERT

How to work out brackets

Example

Imagine that you have bags containing coloured discs.
One bag holds red discs and one holds blue discs.
There are not necessarily the same number of discs in each bag.
There are r red discs in each red bag and b blue discs
in each blue bag.
You put a bag of each colour together.
The number of discs is $(r + b)$.
You then make three identical piles.
You have $3 \times (r + b)$ or $(r + b) \times 3$ or $3(r + b)$.

Examples

If $a = 5$, $b = 3$ and $c = -2$, work out the value of each expression.
- $3(b + 2a) = 3(3 + 10) = 3 \times 13 = 39$
- $(c + a) - (b + a) = (-2 + 5) - (3 + 5) = 3 - 8 = -5$
- $2c + 4(a + c) = 2 \times -2 + 4(5 + -2) = -4 + 4(3) = -4 + 12 = 8$
- $3c - a = 3 \times -2 - 5 = -6 - 5 = -11$

Equations in algebra

Examples

Solve these equations.

a	$a + 3 = 10$	$a = 10 - 3 = 7$
b	$b - 2 = 12$	$b = 12 + 2 = 14$
c	$2c = 10$	$c = 10 \div 2 = 5$
d	$\frac{d}{2} = 4$	$d = 4 \times 2 = 8$
e	$4e = 6$	$e = 6 \div 4 = 1.5$
f	$f + 3 = 0$	$f = 0 - 3 = -3$

Example

Solve this equation for c.
$2c + 5 = 11$
Using a function box, this equation
becomes:

$$c \xrightarrow{\times 2} 2c \xrightarrow{+5} 2c + 5 \longrightarrow 11$$

To 'undo' this equation, the process is:
$(11 - 5) \div 2 = 3 \quad \Rightarrow \quad c = 3$
Check that this works. $3 \times 2 + 5 = 11$

Exercise 3

Work out the value of this expression. $a = 5, b = 3, c - 2$
$2(a + 2c) - (2b + a)$

Exercise 4

Solve the following equations.
1. $2x + 5 = 17$
2. $5y - 3 = 17$

Tactics

Remember that the
answer to an equation
may be positive or
negative, and may
include a fraction
or decimal.

Brackets are important. If $r = 7$ and $b = 3$, then
$(7 + 3) \times 2 = 10 \times 2 = 20$ whereas $7 + 3 \times 2 = 7 + 6 = 13$.

You can solve all equations of this sort by this reversing process.
It is usually easier to do one step at a time.

> **Example**
> Solve this equation for d.
> $$3d - 2 = 19$$
> $$3d = 19 + 2$$
> $$3d = 21$$
> $$d = 21 \div 3$$
> $$d = 7$$

How to solve problems using algebra

> **Example**
> Robert is five years older than his brother and half as old as his sister.
> Robert is n years old. Write expressions for the ages of his brother and sister.
> If the total of their combined ages is 19, form an equation and solve it to find the age of each.
> Robert is n years old.
> His brother is $n - 5$ years old.
> His sister is $2n$ years old.
> $$n + n - 5 + 2n = 19$$
> $$4n - 5 = 19$$
> $$4n = 24$$
> $$n = 6$$
> Robert is six years old, his brother is one year old and his sister is twelve years old.

> **Example**
> A rubber costs m pence. A pencil costs twice as much as a rubber.
> A pen costs three times as much as a pencil.
> I buy a rubber, a pencil and a pen and have 24p left. If I had £2.04 at the start, how much did each cost?
> The rubber costs m pence.
> The pencil costs $2m$ pence.
> The pen costs $6m$ pence.
> $$m + 2m + 6m + 24 = 204$$
> $$9m + 24 = 204$$
> $$9m = 204 - 24$$
> $$9m = 180$$
> $$m = 20$$
>
> The rubber costs 20p.
> The pencil costs 40p.
> The pen costs £1.20.
> *Check*: 20p + 40p + £1.20 + 24p = £2.04.

Exercise 5

1 A girl has e CDs. her friend has 15 more than she has. Her sister has five fewer than she has. If their combined total of CDs is 220, how many does she have?

2 William draws a square with each side r cm long. Anna draws a square with each side 4 cm longer than William's square.
   a Write an expression for the length of one side of Anna's square.
   b Write an expression for the perimeter of Anna's square.
   c If the perimeter of Anna's square is 56 cm, write an equation to show this information and solve it to find the length of William's square.

ERT RED ALERT RED ALERT! RED ALERT RED ALERT

Using equations

Sometimes you will have to solve equations where the letter standing for the number you are trying to find appears on both sides of the equation.

Example

Solve this equation.

$5x + 3 = 2x + 12$

Rearrange the equation until all the letters are on one side of the equation and all the numbers without letters are on the other.

$5x + 3 = 2x + 12$ If it helps, write an instruction for both sides of the equation.

$5x + 3 = 2x + 12$ $(- 2x)$ Subtract $2x$ from both sides of the equation..

$3x + 3 = 12$ $(- 3)$ Subtract 3 from both sides of the equation.

$3x = 9$ $(÷ 3)$

$x = 3$

Check: $5 \times 3 + 3 = 2 \times 3 + 12$

Example

Solve this equation.

$4y - 10 = 2y - 3$ $(- 2y)$

$2y - 10 = -3$ $(+ 10)$ Remember, the sign goes with the letter or number which immediately follows it, so you need -3.

$2y = -3 + 10$

$2y = 7$

$y = 3.5$

Check:

LHS $= 4 \times 3.5 - 10 = 14 - 10 = 4$

RHS $= 2 \times 3.5 - 3 = 7 - 3 = 4$

As both sides are equal 4, the solution is correct.

Exercise 1

Solve these equations.

1   $2a + 11 = a + 16$

(Remember, a is the same as $1a$.)

2   $3v + 2 = v - 6$

(The answer to this equation is negative.)

3   $8t + 7 = 2t + 10$

(The answer to this equation is less than one.)

Tactics

Take care with signs!

ALERT   **Answers to equations can also be negative or less than one.**   RED ALERT RE

Examples

- The length of the rectangle is 2 cm more than its width. If its perimeter is 24 cm, form an equation in w and solve it to find the length and width of the rectangle.

$$2w + 2(w + 2) = 24$$
$$2w + 2w + 4 = 24$$
$$4w + 4 = 24$$
$$4w = 20$$
$$w = 5$$

The length is 7 cm and the width is 5 cm.

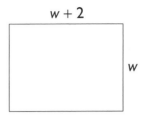

$w + 2$

w

Diagram not drawn to scale

- The length of the shortest side of this triangle is c cm.
  The other two sides are 7 cm and 8 cm longer. Write expressions for the lengths of the other sides in cm.
  The perimeter of the triangle is 30 cm. Write an equation with this information and use it to find out the length of each side.
  The other sides are $c + 7$cm and $c + 8$ cm.

$$c + c + 7 + c + 8 = 30$$
$$3c + 15 = 30$$
$$3c = 30 - 15 = 15$$
$$c = 5$$

The sides are 5 cm, 12 cm and 13 cm.

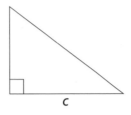

c

Diagram not drawn to scale

Exercise 2

1   The shortest side of a triangle is d cm. The other sides are $d + 2$ cm and $2d - 2$ cm.
    If the perimeter is 24 cm, find the length of each side. (Hint: $d + d + 2 + 2d - 2 = 24$).

2   Kevin is m years old. His sister is 3 years younger. If the sum of their ages is 21 years, write an equation and find Kevin's age.

Tactics

You can use any letter you like for unknowns.

Trial and improvement

Sometimes it is impossible to find an exact solution to a question.

An approximate answer is often quite adequate. One means of approximating is to use trial and improvement.
Start with a rough estimate of the value, then modify that estimate, increasing or decreasing it until the answer is close enough.

> **Examples**
> - £1.00 ÷ 3 = £0.33333...
> - The square root of 2 = 1.414 213 562...

Example

$w^3 + w = 20$. Find w correct to 1 d.p.
Try a value for w. Record your trials as shown.

```
10                                                    30
├─────────────────────────────────────────────────────┤
2                                                      3
too small                                          too big
```

w	$w^3 + w$	Total	Comment
3	27 + 3	30	too big, try smaller
2	8 + 2	10	too small, try bigger
2.5	$2.5^3 + 2.5$	18.125	too small, try bigger
2.9	$2.9^3 + 2.9$	27.289	too big, try a value between 2.5 and 2.9.
2.6	$2.6^3 + 2.6$	20.176	just too big, try 2.55
2.55	$2.55^3 + 2.55$	19.131	too small

Keep trying values and writing them on the line as shown until you find the best approximation.

```
10                     18.125              27.289  30
├──────────────────────┼──────┬──────────────┼─────┤
2                     2.5    2.6           2.9    3
too                   too    just          too   too
small                 small  too           big   big
                             big
```

$2.6^3 + 2.6 = 20.176 = 20.2$ to 1 d.p. and $w = 2.6$ is the best approximation.

Exercise 1

Find all values for x in this exercise correct to 1 d.p.
1 $x^3 - x = 10$
2 $x(x + 1) = 59$

> **Tactics**
>
> The solution to the example above lies between the two values 2.55 and 2.6, but they are both 2.6 to 1 d.p. so, $w = 2.6$ is the best answer.

Sequences

A sequence is a pattern of numbers that follow a rule.

> ## Examples
> Look for the pattern in each sequence, then fill in the missing numbers.
> - 3, 7, 11, … , 19   Add 4 each time.
> - 1, 2, 4, 8, … , 32   Multiply by 2.
> - 4, 5, 7, 10, 14, … , 25   Add 1, add 2, add 3, …
> - 13, 10, 7, 4, 1, …   Subtract 3 each time.
> - 1, 4, 9, … , 25   Add 1, add 3, add 5, … or use square numbers, 1×1, 2×2, …

What does the nth term mean?

The first sequence from the example can be written in table form.

Position n	1	2	3	4	5	…
Value t	3	7	11	?	19	…

The number in the first position is the first term. The number in the second position is the second term, and so on. It's easy to supply the fourth term by adding $11 + 4 = 15$. If the question had asked for the eighth term, it would be easy to count on and find the answer 31. However, if you were asked for the ninetieth term, you might decide that you could find better things to do with your time than spending it counting on in fours.

The rule for finding the nth term of this sequence is $4n - 1$, giving the rule $t = 4n - 1$.
That troublesome ninetieth term would be $4 \times 90 - 1 = 359$.

> ## Examples
> Give the first three terms and the hundredth term of each sequence.
> - $3n + 1$ $3 \times 1 + 1 = 4$, $3 \times 2 + 1 = 7$, $3 \times 3 + 1 = 10$, $3 \times 100 + 1 = 301$
> - $2n - 1$ $2 \times 1 - 1 = -1$, $2 \times 2 - 1 = 3$, $2 \times 3 - 1 = 5$, $2 \times 100 - 1 = 199$
> - $4n + 2$ $4 \times 1 + 2 = 6$, $4 \times 2 + 2 = 10$, $4 \times 3 + 2 = 14$, $4 \times 100 + 2 = 402$
> - $5n$ $5 \times 1 = 5$, $5 \times 2 = 10$, $5 \times 3 = 15$, $5 \times 100 = 500$
> - n^2 $1 \times 1 = 1$, $2 \times 2 = 4$, $3 \times 3 = 9$, $100 \times 100 = 10\,000$

Exercise 1

Give the first three terms and the fiftieth term of these sequences.

1 $3n + 5$
2 $7n - 6$
3 $\,n - 6$

Tactics

Having a rule for the nth term saves a lot of bother.

RED ALERT   Although you could use any letter, normally n is taken to stand for any term. You may see the term called t.

Mappings, equations and graphs

Mappings

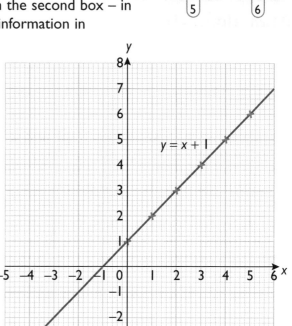

The right-hand box in the diagram shows the result of adding 1 to any number in the left-hand box. This is called a **mapping**.

You can write a formula for the same information. If x represents the number in the left-hand box, then the formula is $x + 1$.

If you choose a letter to stand for the number in the second box – in maths you often use y – then you can write the information in equation form.

$y = x + 1$

The same information can be shown on a graph.

Note that you should:
- label the axes
- join the points with a straight line, using a ruler
- extend the line beyond the values given
- label the equation line, starting with $y = .$

Exercise 1

Look at the graphs.
Compare them with the graph above
and work out the equations of the lines.
Use mapping diagrams if it helps.

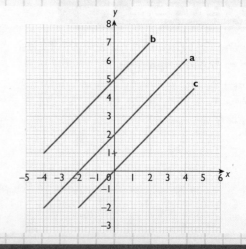

Equations and graphs

In this work x is always the starting value and y is the finishing value.
The function machine shows a blueprint for an equation.

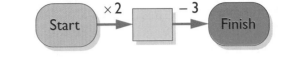

If the starting value is x and the output is y, what is the equation?

Answer: $2x - 3 = y$

We can show these results in a table of values.

x	-3	-2	-1	0	1	2	3
$2x$	-6	-4	-2	0	2	4	6
-3	-3	-3	-3	-3	-3	-3	-3
$y = 2x - 3$	-9	-7	-5	-3	-1	1	3

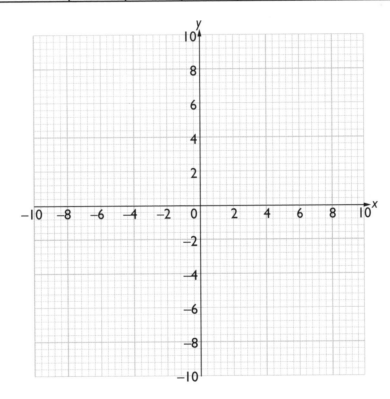

Exercise 2

Mark the points for $y = 2x - 3$ from the table above on the graph, and join them up. If you are correct, your graph should be a straight line.

Tactics

All graphs which have x or $-x$ with or without another number added or subtracted can be represented as a straight-line on a graph.
The equations of some lines are very common and worth recognising.

43

The graph of $y = x$

Draw a set of axes and label them x and y in the usual way.
Number each axis from −5 to 5.
The equation $y = x$ means that both x and y have the same
value. if $x = 1$ then $y = 1$, if $x = -1$, then $y = -1$ and so on.
Plot the points on the graph and join up the line. It should
look like the diagram opposite. The point $(0, 0)$ is the origin.

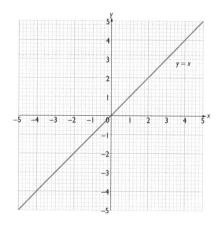

The graph of $x = ?$

Look at the graph opposite.
What are the coordinates of A, B and C?
$A = (2, 1)$, $B = (2, 3)$, $C = (2, -2)$
What do you notice about the x-coordinate?
The value of x is always 2.
The equation of the line is $x = 2$.

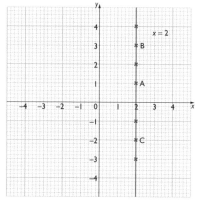

The graph of $y = ?$

Look at the graph opposite.
What are the coordinates of D, E and F?
What do you notice about the y-coordinate?
$D = (-2, -2)$, $E = (1, -2)$, $F = (2, -2)$
The value of y is always −2.
The equation of the line is $y = -2$.
Graphs of this form are always straight lines.
The line $x = ?$ is vertical and the line $y = ?$ is horizontal.

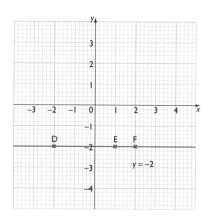

Exercise 3

1 David draws the graph of $y = 6$.
What should the y co-ordinate
be when x is
a 7 b −2 c 0 ?

2 Anne draws the graph of $x = -8$.
What should the x co-ordinate be
when y is
a 3 b −4 c 0 ?

Tactics

If you find this confusing, pick
three pairs of coordinates on a
horizontal or vertical line.
Check their x-values and their
y-values to see which ones
stay the same.

ALERT! RED ALERT RED ALERT RED ALERT RED

The first diagram on the opposite page shows the line $y = x$.
This is the table of values for $y = 2x$.

$y = 2x$						
x	-1	0	1	2	3	4
$y = 2x$	-2	0	2	4	6	8

The diagram shows the equation $y = 2x$.
Use the graph to check that the values in
the table are correct.

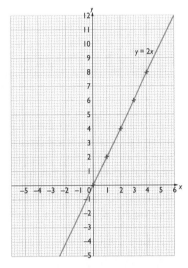

These are the tables and graphs for $y = 3x$ and $y = 4x$.

$y = 3x$						
x	-1	0	1	2	3	4
$y = 3x$	-3	0	3	6	9	12

$y = 4x$						
x	-1	0	1	2	3	4
$y = 4x$	-4	0	4	8	12	16

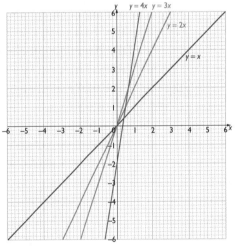

The graph shows the lines $y = x$, $y = 2x$, $y = 3x$, $y = 4x$.

Exercise 4

1 Using the graph above, what do you
notice about the lines as the multiple
of x gets bigger?
2 What would the line look like
if the multiple of x were a fraction
less than one.?

Tactics

⚠

Always use a sharp pencil when
you are drawing graphs.

RT   **Graphs which show multiples of x are straight lines.
Check carefully when you draw them.**   RED ALERT

Organise your memory

Even a favourite subject can have its downside, and that is often the amount of things that have to be learned. Learning vocabulary or verb endings in a foreign language, memorising formulae in maths and science, and trying to cope with the unexpected in English spelling can be a chore, but having to go over them time after time is boring and frustrating. Fortunately, there are various tips that might rescue you.

• Rhymes, mnemonics and sayings can be very useful memory joggers for all sorts of subjects. In maths, a way to remember the area of a circle is to say to yourself, 'πr squarea gives you the area.' You can remember that 'necessary' has one c and two s's because we wear one collar and two socks. You have probably heard of others, but the most easily remembered memory joggers are the ones you invent yourself. They can be stupid, funny or even incredibly rude, as long as you keep the rude ones to yourself.

- Try 'clumping' information together. This cuts down on the time spent and helps everything to hang together. For instance, if you are learning a foreign language, and have to learn the word for 'hear', make a note of 'hearing', 'heard' and maybe 'ear', if it's related. Try to remember how to say, 'Where is the....?' or 'I should like....' and you will be able to make up hundreds of different sentences by putting a different word on the end.

- If you have a very factual subject – the causes of the first world war, how a blast furnace works, the bones of the hand – note how many facts you need to remember, and then see if you can make up an acronym to help you. (An acronym is a group of letters, usually an abbreviation for something, or a set of initials. For instance USA is an acronym for United States of America.)

- You can learn lists by setting them to music. Lists aren't fussy. The music can be pop or classical and the words don't have to rhyme.

- Memory joggers don't have to be verbal. Try drawing little pictures or designing logos to give some variety.

How to label lines and shapes

Straight lines and angles

Angles are formed when lines meet or cross each other.

$a + b = 180°$

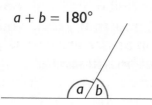

$c + d + e = 180°$

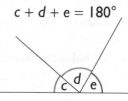

$4f = 180°$

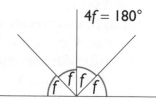

Intersecting lines and angles

Angles that meet at a point add up to 360°.

$g + h = 180°$
$2g + 2h = 360°$

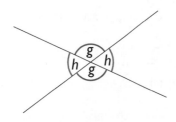

$j + k + l + m + n = 360°$

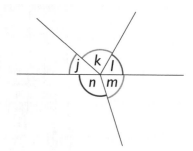

Exercise 1

Using algebra and the diagrams above, complete the following. The first has been done for you.

1   $180° - b = \square$ $180° - b = a$

2   $180° - e = \square + \square$

2   $f = 180° \div e = \square = \square$

4   $j + k + l = \square + \square$

Parallel lines and angles

Angles formed when a straight line crosses parallel lines have special properties.

Alternate (**Z**) angles are equal.

Corresponding (**F**) angles are equal.

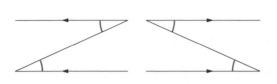
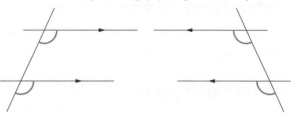

Angles in triangles

Use three-letter notation for angles. The centre letter is at the point of the angle and the outside letters are at the ends of the arms of the angle. The angle labelled w in the diagram is angle JLK or angle KLJ (also known as ∠JLK or ∠KLJ). The angle labelled z is ∠MJL or ∠LJM.

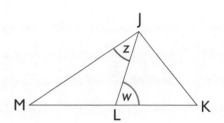

Example
Triangle ABC is isosceles, with AB = AC and ∠ABC = 70°.
D is the midpoint of AB and E is the midpoint of AC. DE is parallel to BC.
Find the size of:
a ∠ACB   **b** ∠AED   **c** ∠BAC

a ∠ACB = ∠ABC = 70° (triangle ABC is isosceles, AB = AC)
b ∠AED = ∠ACB = 70° (corresponding angles)
c ∠BAC = 40° (180° − 140°)

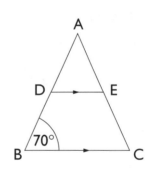

Exercise 2

Using the diagram from the example above, find the size of each of these angles. Give a reason for your answer.

1 ∠DEC
2 ∠DBC + ∠BCE + ∠DEC + ∠EDB

Tactics
The diagrams on this page are not accurately drawn. This means that you can't find the right answer by measuring. Look out for the same comment on exam papers.

ERT   **Make sure you know how to recognise different types of triangle.**   RED ALERT RED ALERT

Polygons

Understanding the jargon

A polygon is any straight-sided two-dimensional shape.
In regular polygons all the sides are equal and all the angles are equal.

Common polygons

Here are some polygons that you will often use in maths.

Symmetry

If a shape has line symmetry, a line can be drawn through it, splitting it into two identical halves, each the mirror image of the other. This line is called a reflection line, a mirror line or an axis of symmetry. Some shapes have more than one reflection line.

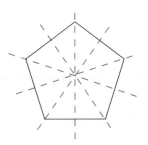 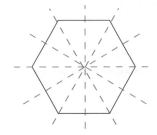 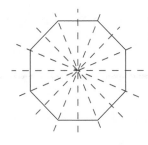

Exercise 1

How many lines of symmetry does each shape have?

1	a square	2	a rectangle	3	a regular pentagon
4	a regular hexagon	5	a regular octagon	6	a circle

RED ALERT! Apart from the rectangle the shapes in the exercise above are regular. Irregular shapes may not have as many lines of symmetry. **RED**

Example

The diagram shows a hexagon with FC and XZ as lines of symmetry.
∠ABC = 150°, ∠AFE = 60°, Y is the centre of rotation.

Work out the following angles.

a ∠AFC　　**b** ∠CDE

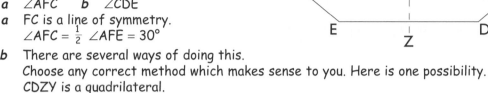

a FC is a line of symmetry.
∠AFC = $\frac{1}{2}$ ∠AFE = 30°

b There are several ways of doing this.
Choose any correct method which makes sense to you. Here is one possibility.
CDZY is a quadrilateral.
∠DZY = ∠CYZ = 90° (YZ and CY are lines of symmetry)
∠DCB = ∠AFE = 60°
∠DCY = 30° (FC is a line of symmetry)
90° + 90° + 30° = 210°
360° − 210° = 150°
∠CDE = 150°

When a polygon is irregular, although the sum of the angles remains the same, the interior angles are not usually the same.

A rectangle is an exemption to this rule because each interior angle is 90°, as is each interior angle of a square.

Exercise 2

1 Find the size of ∠BXY.
2 If you cut the hexagon along the lines FC and XZ what would be the shape of any one of the four pieces?

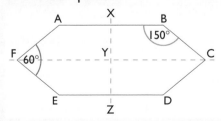

> **Tactics**
>
> This hexagon is irregular. It does not have 6 lines of symmetry.

51

Quadrilaterals

A quadrilateral is any two-dimensional four-sided shape.
Some quadrilaterals are very common.

	Name	Sides	Angles
	square	all sides equal and opposite sides parallel	each angle = 90°
	rectangle	opposite sides equal and parallel	each angle = 90°
	parallelogram	opposite sides equal and parallel	opposite angles equal
	rhombus	all sides equal opposite sides equal and parallel diagonals cross at right angles	opposite angles equal
	kite	two pairs of adjacent sides equal diagonals cross at right angles	angles between non-equal sides equal
	trapezium	one pair of unequal sides parallel	

Exercise 3

Fill in the spaces.

1   A quadrilateral with opposite sides equal and parallel could be a _____ ,
   a _____ , a _____ or a _____ .
2   A quadrilateral whose diagonals cross at right angles could be a _____ ,
   or a _____ .
3   A quadrilateral with all angles equal is a _____ or a _____ .

Quadrilaterals and symmetry

Line or reflection symmetry
Many quadrilaterals have reflectional or line symmetry.

Shape		Axes of symmetry
	square	4
	rectangle	2
	parallelogram	0 (unless a rhombus)
	rhombus	2
	kite	1
	trapezium	0, or 1 if an isosceles trapezium

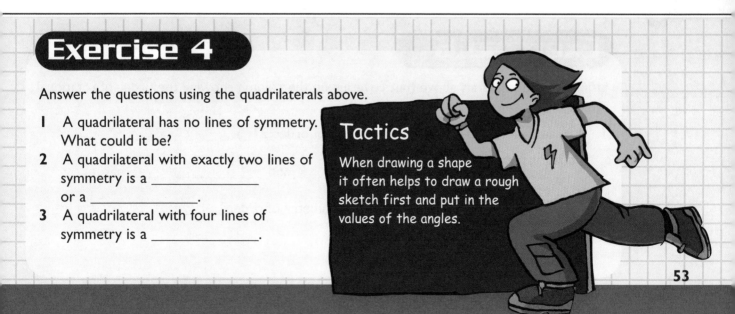

Exercise 4

Answer the questions using the quadrilaterals above.

1   A quadrilateral has no lines of symmetry. What could it be?

2   A quadrilateral with exactly two lines of symmetry is a _____ or a _____.

3   A quadrilateral with four lines of symmetry is a _____.

Tactics

When drawing a shape it often helps to draw a rough sketch first and put in the values of the angles.

Rotational symmetry

The number of ways in which a shape can be turned, or rotated and still fit exactly over its initial position is called its order of rotation. If a shape can only be in one position without changing, it has rotational symmetry of order 1.

It sometimes helps to use tracing paper to work out the order of symmetry of a shape. Put the paper over the shape, and trace it. Then put your pencil on the spot where you think the centre should be. If you are right, you can swivel the shape round so that although another side comes to the top, the tracing of the shape in its starting position is identical to the shape in its new position.

Shape	Order of rotational symmetry
square	4
rectangle	2
parallelogram	1
rhombus	2
kite	1
trapezium	1

Exercise 5

Using the quadrilaterals above (but covering up the column showing the order of rotational symmetry), answer the following questions.

1 A quadrilateral with rotational symmetry of order 2 is a _____ or a _____ .

2 A _____ , _____ and _____ have rotational symmetry of order 1.

3 A _____ has rotational symmetry of order _____ .

Congruent shapes and shapes that tessellate

Understanding the jargon

Congruent shapes are identical. That means that they will fit on top of each other even though you may have to turn one of them round or flip it over to make it fit.
Shapes that fit together round a point, with no gaps, tessellate.

Making patterns

Shapes that tessellate can be used, on their own or with other shapes, to make patterns.
See how many different shapes you can identify in this pattern. Note the shapes that
are congruent.

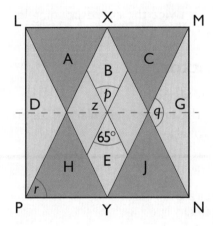

Exercise 6

Study the diagram of tessellating shapes and tiles, then answer these questions,
LMNP is a square. X is the midpoint of LM and Y is the midpoint of PN. Z is the centre
of the square.

1 Find the size of angles p, q and r.
2 If you rotated shape B through 180° around the centre of the tile, which piece would it cover?
3 Name another triangle which is congruent to triangle C.
4 What name is given to the shape E?
5 What transformation would you need to move triangle G to triangle D?

RT RED ALERT RED ALERT! RED ALERT RED ALERT

Enlargement

Understanding the jargon

In any transformation, the original shape is the object and the transformed (enlarged) shape is the image.

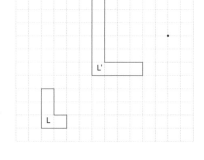

What is enlargement?

In an enlargement, every length in the object is multiplied by the same amount to produce the image. This is called the multiplier or scale factor.

In the diagram, every length in L′ is twice the corresponding length in shape L.
So L′ is an enlargement of shape L with a scale factor 2.

How to find a scale factor

Measure one length in the original shape.
Find the corresponding length in the image (the enlarged form) and measure it.
Divide the new length by the original.

Example

S′ is an enlargement of the square S.
The scale factor of the enlargement is 6.
The perimeter of the square S is 4×1
$= 4$ cm
The perimeter of the enlarged square S′
$= 4 \times 6 = 24$ cm
The area of the square $S = 1$ cm^2
The area of the enlarged square S′
$= 6 \times 6 = 36$ cm^2

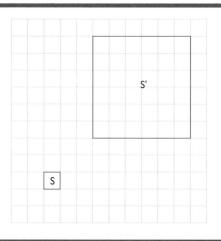

Exercise 1

1 A square with sides 5 cm is enlarged by a scale factor of 3.
   What is the length of each side of the new square?

2 What was the perimeter of the original square?

3 What is the perimeter of the new square?

Tactics

Enlargements are $\dfrac{New}{Old}$

Remember: Enlargements are novel! New OVEr oLd.

Triangle ABC has been enlarged from centre A to A'B'C'. The line AXY is an axis of symmetry.

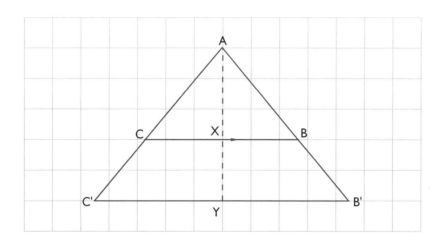

Example
a   What is the scale factor of the enlargement?
b   If AB was 12 cm long, how long would A'B' be?
c   If B'C' were 20 cm long, how long would BC be?
d   If ∠ABC = 53° to the nearest degree, what is the size of ∠AB'C'?

a   Each line is twice as long as the original line, so the scale factor is 2.
b   12 × 2 = 24 cm
c   20 ÷ 2 = 10 or $\frac{1}{2}$ × 20 = 10
d   Angles remain the same when a shape is enlarged. ∠AB'C' = 53°

Exercise 2

Refer to the diagram at the top of the page to answer these questions.
1   Name a triangle which is congruent to triangle AC'Y.
2   Name a triangle which is an enlargement of triangle AXB.

Tactics

Enlargements are not congruent to the original shapes as they are not identical in size, although they are the same shape.

ERT RED ALERT RED ALERT! RED ALERT RED ALERT

Circles

Understanding the jargon

The circumference is the distance all round the outside of a circle. In other shapes it is called the perimeter.
A diameter is any line which crosses a circle from one side to the other, passing through the centre of the circle,
A radius is half a diameter. It is a line joining the centre of a circle to a point on the circumference.
The plural or radius is radii – not radiuses!

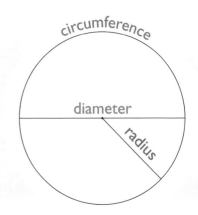

Understanding π

In any circle, the circumference is slightly more than three times the diameter.

It's impossible to measure exactly the 'and a bit'.

Press the π button on your calculator. You may get something like 3.141 592 654 … . And that's not the end of the story.
Even if your calculator could give you a million decimal places, you would not reach the end of π. It goes on for ever and ever and ever … .

Usually we can shorten π to 3.14. It's a good idea to get used to using the π button on your calculator as soon as possible, though.

If you have a mental arithmetic question involving π, you won't be allowed your trusty calculator, so use a value of 3 instead. Such a question would ask for an approximate answer.

The circumference of a circle

The formula for finding the circumference, C, of a circle is $\pi \times$ diameter. $C = \pi d$
As the diameter is twice the radius, you may see the formula written as: $C = 2\pi r$

Exercise 1

Using the π button on your calculator, find the circumference of the following circles to 1 d.p.

1 Diameter 2.5 cm
2 Diameter 3.8 cm
3 Radius 7.1 cm
4 Radius 2.6 cm

Tactics

π is used to represent this number.
(It's better than writing a million or more digits and still not finishing.)
Sometimes π is given as $\frac{22}{7}$.
Try working out 22 ÷ 7 on your calculator.

RED ALERT! **Remember, a sketch illustrates an idea. It is not meant to be accurate.** RED ALERT RED

The area of a circle

To find the area of a circle, you square the length of the radius and multiply the result by π.
The formula for finding the area, A, of a circle is usually written as $\pi \times r^2$ or $A = \pi r^2$.

Which formula is which?

Many people can remember the two formulae, but they forget which one is for the area and which is for the circumference. A clue is that area always involves squared units, so πr^2 is the formula for the area.

Examples

Use the π button on your calculator to find the circumference of each of these circles.
Give all answers correct to 1 d.p.
- Diameter 3.2 m   Circumference = $\pi \times D$ = 10.1 m
- Diameter 7.9 cm   Circumference = $\pi \times D$ = 24.8 cm
- Radius 4.3 m   If the radius = 4.3 m, the diameter = 4.3 × 2 = 8.6 m
  Circumference = $\pi \times D$ = 27.02 = 27.0 m to 1 d.p.
  Remember to write the zero, as the answer has to be correct to 1 d.p.
- Radius 7.4 m   Circumference = $2\pi \times r$ = 46.5 m
- Diameter 2.1 m   Circumference = $\pi \times D$ = 6.6 m

Examples

Mrs Patel wants to make a new flower bed in her garden. She has drawn a sketch of her garden with the new flower bed marked.
- What is the diameter of the flower bed?
  15 – 4 = 11 m   Diameter = 11 m
- What is the radius?
  Radius = 11 ÷ 2 = 5.5 m
- What is the area of the whole garden?
  15 × 20 = 300 m²
- What is the area of the flower bed?
  Area of flower bed = $\pi r^2 = \pi \times 5.5^2$ = 95 m²
- What area of the garden will not be used for the new flower bed?
  300 – 95 = 205 m²

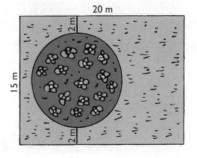

Exercise 2

Find the areas of the following circles.
Give all answers to 1 d.p.

1 Radius 4.6 cm
2 Radius 7.8 cm
3 Diameter 5.6 cm
4 Diameter 5.3 m
5 Diameter 2.9 m

Tactics

Another way is to say to yourself, 'area is squared'.
Maybe this diagram will help you to remember the formula for the circumference.
Circumference = πD

RT   **You need the radius to work out the area.**
   Halve the diameter to get the radius.   RED ALERT RED ALERT

Area

Area

Squares and rectangles
area = length × width (The width is sometimes called the breadth.)

Parallelograms
ED and BD cross at right angles.
They are perpendicular.
The area of parallelogram ACDE = area of rectangle CBDE
$$= ED \times BD$$
The area of a parallelogram = base × perpendicular height

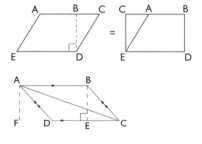

Triangles

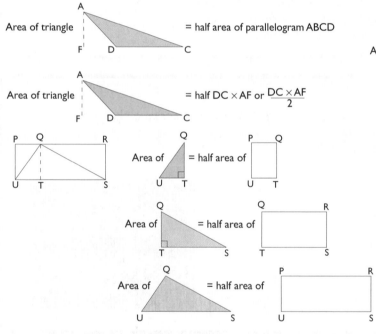

Area of triangle = half area of parallelogram ABCD

Area of triangle = half DC × AF or $\dfrac{DC \times AF}{2}$

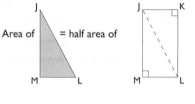

Area of = half area of

The formula for finding the area of any triangle is:

$\Delta = \frac{1}{2} \times$ base × height or

$\Delta = \dfrac{\text{base} \times \text{height}}{2}$

Exercise 1

1 A rectangle has an area of 24 cm².
   If the length of the rectangle is 8 cm,
   find the width.

2 The rectangle in question 1 is cut
   diagonally. What is the area of each
   of the triangles?

3 A right-angled triangle has an area of
   10 cm². If the base of the triangle is
   4 cm, find the height.

Tactics

Always start by finding two
perpendicular lines when you
are trying to work out an area.

How to find the area of an isosceles triangle

Triangles which have two sides equal and two angles the same size are isosceles triangles.
Most isosceles triangles do not include a right angle or line of symmetry.
You have to draw one in like this. Turn the page round if it makes it easier to spot the two sides which are the same length.

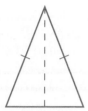  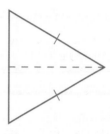

How to find the area of an equilateral triangle

Equilateral triangles have all sides equal and all angles equal.

To find the area of an equilateral triangle, you can treat it as if it were isosceles, and draw the perpendicular height from one vertex (corner).

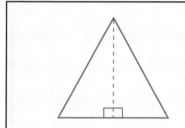 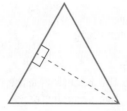 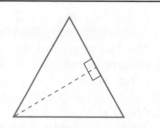

Exercise 2

1 The perimeter of an equilateral triangle is 27 cm. How long is each side?
2 An isosceles triangle has a base of 10 cm and a height of 12 cm. What is its area?
3 A parallelogram is cut across diagonally. What sort of triangles would it make?

Tactics

You can always find a perpendicular in an isosceles or equilateral triangle by drawing a line from the vertex of the two equal sides to the midpoint of the opposite side.

ERT RED ALERT RED ALERT! RED ALERT RED ALERT

Area of composite shapes

Understanding the jargon

Composite shapes are made up of two or more simple shapes. The easiest way to find the area is to split them up.

Example

The racetrack ABCD is a rectangle with semicircular ends.
a   Find the perimeter of the shape.
b   Find the area of the shape.

a   The two semicircular ends would make a
    complete circle if they were placed together.
    Diameter = width of the rectangle
             = 13 m
    Circumference = $\pi \times D$
                  = 40.84 m
    The two lengths of the rectangle complete
    the perimeter.
    Perimeter = 40.84 + 60 = 100.84 m
                          = 101 m to the nearest metre.
b   Area = area of rectangle + area of two semicircles
    Area of rectangle = 30×13
                      = 390 m²
    Area of two semicircles = area of circle
                            = $\pi \times 6.5^2 = 132.73$ m²
    Total area = 390 + 132.73
               = 522.73 m²
               = 523 m² to the nearest m².

Exercise 1

1   Using the racetrack above, but with AB = 40 m and BC = 15 m, find:
    a the perimeter of the shape.
    b the area of the shape.

Give your answers to 2 d.p.

Example

The floorplan of a room. EFGH, is a square with a semicircle on each side.
Find the area of the floor.
Remember, 20 m is the diameter.
Area = area of square + area of two circles
Area of square = 400 m^2
Area of circles = $\pi r^2 \times 2$ = 628 m^2
Total floor area = 400 + 628 = 1028 m^2

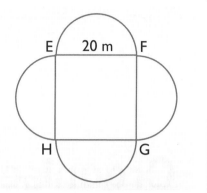

Sometimes it is easier to block in parts of the diagram to make a simpler shape, and then subtract the extra amount.

Example

Find the area of this shape.

The easiest way to solve this is to block in the rest of the square.
Area of complete square = 144 cm^2
Area of shaded sections = $4 \times 4 \times 2$ = 32 cm^2
Required area = 144 − 32 = 112 cm^2

Exercise 2

1 Using the diagram at the top of this page,
   but with EF = FG = GH = HE = 30 m, find:
   a the perimeter.
   b the area.

   Give your answers to 2 d.p.

Tactics

Always show your working, as you may score some marks even if the final answer is wrong.

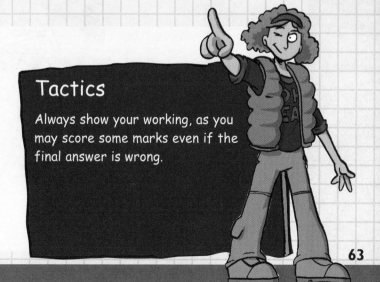

RT RED ALERT RED ALERT! RED ALERT RED ALERT

5

Organise your revision

You may find that you have more tests or exams this year than in earlier years, and some of them have an effect on your future, such as which set you are put in. Start revising in good time. Leaving it all to the night before won't work!

- Make a revision plan. This is easy if you are revising for a test in just one subject, but gets complicated if you have exams in most subjects. To make a workable plan, you need to take each subject in turn and break it down into manageable chunks. If you start about a month before the exams – or before, if you feel like it, or realise that it's necessary – you should be able to split up the work so that it doesn't wear you down. Allow yourself some spare time and flexibility. Almost certainly, something unexpected will turn up so you won't be able to keep rigidly to your plan. If you have built in some room for manoeuvre, you can still catch up and get back on course.

- Remember to look back over your work from time to time, so that you keep your new knowledge firmly at the front of your mind. This may sound like a chore, but it does get easier. Eventually all that unfamiliar material becomes commonplace and you will wonder why you struggled with it.

- Try summarising the information that you have to learn on a series of small cards. This task in itself will make you go over your work again and sift out the really important information. Then you merely count the cards and divide them into the number of weeks available. When you think that you know a card, put it into a separate box. You will be surprised how impressive your stock of knowledge soon becomes. About once a week, look through what you have learned, and if you have forgotten anything, put the card back with the pile which you have still to learn.

- If you prefer, you can use a database on computer to design cards or information sheets. The act of designing a database can itself be helpful and, in addition, you can add to or amend it whenever you need.

- Get together with a friend to go over revision notes and to test each other. Choose someone, though, who is of roughly the same standard as you are.

- When you are learning a foreign language, especially vocabulary, try recording yourself. Sometimes that will help a word to stick – even if your accent would make a native speaker cringe!

- All right! You've left everything until the last minute, so what can you do? Obviously, your options are limited, but look through your notes, and go over the most important words or facts with a highlighter pen. Keep looking through these notes in the hope that you will manage to learn enough to get by – and try to be better organised next time.

Frequency diagrams

Discrete and continuous data

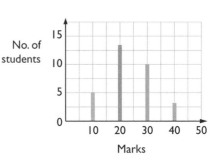

Graph 1
The graph shows the results of a class of students in a French test. It is not sensible to join the points to each other, since it is not possible to record the results of, for example, three and a half students. This is discrete data.

Graph 2
These graphs show the numbers of goals scored by the school football team in its first six matches of the season. As the points should not really be

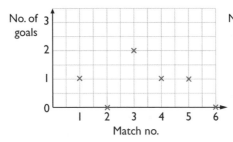 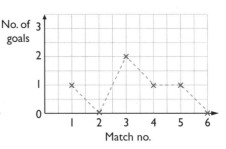

joined, it would be better to use a line graph (see above). You will sometimes see graphs like this, where the points have been joined to make it easier to interpret the results. When the points are joined up, it is better to use a dotted line rather than a solid one.

Graph 3
The temperature in the school playground was measured at hourly intervals on a day in July and the results were shown on a graph. Since the temperature never fell below 20°C, the first part of the vertical (y) axis is not needed. The jagged line shows that the graph has been 'shrunk' to omit it. As temperature rises or falls over a continuous scale, the points are joined with a line. You can read, for example, the approximate temperature after three and a half hours. This is continuous data.

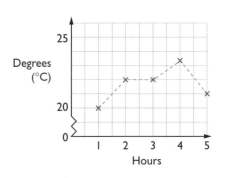

Exercise 1

1   5% of students in a survey chose music as their favourite subject. How many degrees would represent these students on a pie chart?
2   How many degrees on a pie chart would represent 35% of responses?
3   54° represents _____% of responses.

Tactics

We sometimes measure pie charts in degrees and sometimes in percentages. Make sure you know these conversions.

360° = 100%
180° = 50%
90° = 25%
36° = 10%

Example

For each of these situations, say whether you could sensibly join the points on a graph.

a   a patient's temperature chart
b   the number of cars passing a school counted for a specified hour each day
c   the number of students from each class belonging to the gym club
d   the growth in a sunflower plant measured each day at 11 o'clock

You would join the points in a and d. Temperatures and growth are continuous.
You would not join the points in b and c. You can only have whole numbers of cars and people.

Pie charts

Two groups of students from two different classes were asked where they would most like to spend their summer holiday.

Pie charts like this are useful for comparing results and showing trends, but take care not to jump to

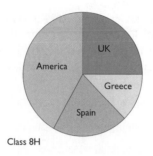

Class 8H

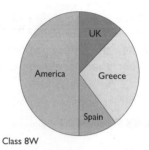

Class 8W

conclusions. You may need more information. If there were 32 students in class 8H, eight of them would prefer the UK for their holiday. If there were 12 students in class 8W, six of them would prefer to holiday in America. The graphs are showing percentages, not numbers. They do not show, for example, that more students from 8W than from 8H chose America.

Example

a   It is not necessarily true that there are more students in class 8H who would prefer to go to Spain than there are in class 8W. Why is this?
b   What percentage of class 8W would prefer to spend their next holiday in America?

a   It depends on the number of students who were asked. If, overall, more students from class 8W than from class 8H were surveyed, then, although the percentage would be smaller, there would be more actual 'votes'.
b   You can see from the diagram that the angle on the pie chart is 180°, which is half of the angle at a point (360°), so the percentage = 50%.

Exercise 2

1   Which was the preferred country for both groups?
2   In class ———, 25% wanted to spend their next holiday in the UK.

Exercise 3

Refer to the pie charts on the right.
Fill in the missing numbers.

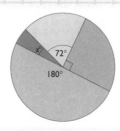

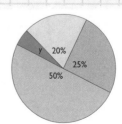

1   $x =$ _____ °
2   $y =$ _____ %
3   72° = _____ %

Scatter diagrams and correlation

Understanding the jargon

A scatter diagram is used to check whether there is a direct link between two sets of data, by plotting the data on a set of coordinate axes.

There is correlation if there is a link or relationship between the points, shown by a trend in the position of the points. If the points lie on a straight line, there is perfect correlation.

When the line of the points appears to rise, from left to right, the correlation is positive.

When the line of the points appears to fall, the correlation is negative.

Correlation

Scatter graph 1

A teacher noted the results gained by the members of his form in their latest French and German tests. He plotted them on a scatter graph. The results appear to indicate that students who are good at French tend to be good at German too, and vice versa. This is an example of positive correlation.

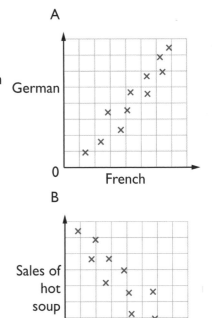

Scatter graph 2

A school tuck shop sells hot and cold snacks. The scatter graph shows the sales of hot soup over a month when the temperature fluctuated. As the temperature rose, the sales of hot soup decreased. This is an example of negative correlation.

Exercise 1

Say whether you would expect positive, negative or no correlation if you drew scatter graphs of the following situations.

1. Sales of woolly hats recorded over a month when the temperature fluctuated.
2. The marks scored in an English test and the number of books read in a month.

Scatter graph 3

Sometimes there is no relationship between the events being studied. No one would expect to see any link or correlation between people's house numbers and their ages.

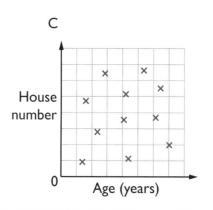

Exam results

Two of these points have been plotted on the graph below.

Student	A	B	C	D	E	F	G	H	I	J	K	L	M	N	O	P
Physics	10	12	7	14	18	4	9	16	2	7	13	5	19	20	18	3
Chemistry	20	34	12	39	42	15	27	44	17	20	31	15	50	20	40	8

Try plotting the remaining points, then use your results in exercise 2 below.

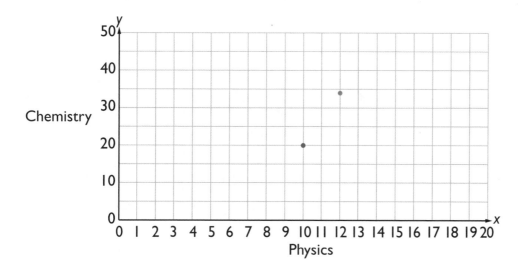

Exercise 2

1 What sort of correlation does this graph appear to show?

2 There are two unexpected results. What are they?

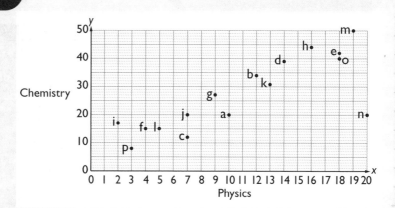

Probability

The diagram shows the results when two dice are thrown and the results are added together.

		First dice					
		1	2	3	4	5	6
Second dice	1	2	3	4	5	6	7
	2	3	4	5	6	7	8
	3	4	5	6	7	8	9
	4	5	6	7	8	9	10
	5	6	7	8	9	10	11
	6	7	8	9	10	11	12

Make sure you can see where the numbers have come from.

When you have two ordinary dice, the number of outcomes is thirty-six, not twelve.

You can always find the number of outcomes by multiplying together all the possibilities of each item.

The number of outcomes if you toss a coin and throw a dice is twelve – two for the coin and six for the die. $2 \times 6 = 12$.

Exercise 1

Using the information above answer the following questions.
Remember to use fractions.
Give each answer in its lowest terms.

1 What is the probability of scoring 6?
2 What is the probability of scoring 10?
3 What total are you most likely to score and what is the probability of scoring it?

Tactics

Brush up on fractions if you want to do well in probability.

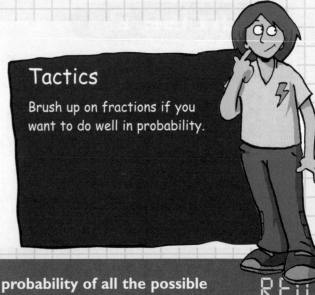

Remember that the total probability of all the possible outcomes is 1.

Example

Spinner 1

Jack

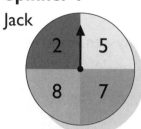

Spinner 2

Paul

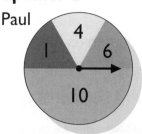

Jack and Paul are playing a game.
Jack is using spinner 1 and Paul is using spinner 2.
Each spins his spinner once.

Fill in the gaps in the sentences.

a _____ is more likely than _____ to score less than 6.

b _____ is more likely than _____ to score 8 or more.

c _____ is more likely than _____ to score an odd number.

d _____ is more likely than _____ to score a multiple of 2.

e It is impossible for_____ to score a prime number.

a Jack is more likely than Paul to score less than 6.

b Paul is more likely than Jack to score 8 or more.

c Jack is more likely than Paul to score an odd number.

d Paul is more likely than Jack to score a multiple of 2.

e It is impossible for Paul to score a prime number.

Exercise 2

Some students were asked about their eating habits.
One of the questions was, 'Did you have chips as part of
your lunch yesterday?' The responses are given in the
table. Give your answers to questions 1, 2 and 3 as decimals to 2 d.p.

	Boys	Girls
Chips	38	12
No chips	12	16

1 What is the probability that a student chosen at random ate chips at lunch yesterday?

2 What is the probability that a student chosen at random from the girls ate chips at lunch yesterday?

3 What is the probability that a student chosen at random from the boys did not eat chips yesterday?

4 What percentage of meals served to this group would you expect to include chips?

5 In 200 meals served to these students, how many would you expect to include chips?

TEST PAPER 1

Mental arithmetic test

If possible, ask someone else to read this test aloud for you. Write your answers down as quickly as you can.

1   A line is twenty millimetres long. How many centimetres is that?

2   When $w = 4$, what is the value of $3w - 2$?

3   What is the order of rotational symmetry of a regular hexagon?

4   What is the cube root of 27?

5   Subtract nine hundred and ninety-eight from four million.

6   A vet said that she had three times as many cats as dogs on her list. If she sees five hundred different dogs and cats in a year, how many cats would you expect her to see?

7   On a pie chart, 90° represents the number of students in a survey who said that they had been to the cinema that week. If 60 students were questioned, how many did the 90° represent?

8   A jacket cost £45.00. Its price was reduced in a sale by 10%. What was the new price?

9   Find the product of 20 and 300.

10   How many 50 pence pieces could you exchange for £17.50?

11   If $a = 10$ and $b = 4$, find the value of $a^2 - b^2$.

12   A square has an area of 36 cm². What is its perimeter?

13   Write down an approximate area for a circle with a diameter of 8 m.

14   The formula for a sequence is $t = 3n + 1$. What is the value of the fifth term?

15   What is the area of a triangle with a base of 5 cm and a perpendicular height of 4 cm?

16   If the probability of choosing a chocolate from a bag of sweets is 0.65, what is the probability of *not* choosing a chocolate?

17   Rachel thought of a number, doubled it and added one. The answer was 15. What number did she think of?

18   How many metres are the same as 3.5 km?

19   Simplify $3t + 4t - t$.

20   What is the smallest number into which 4, 5 and 6 will each divide without a remainder?

Responses

1 _____

2 _____

3 _____

4 _____

5 _____

6 _____

7 _____

8 _____

9 _____

10 _____

11 _____

12 _____

13 _____

14 _____

15 _____

16 _____

17 _____

18 _____

19 _____

20 _____

TEST PAPER 2

Time allowed: 1 hour

Do not use a calculator for this paper.

1   The diagram shows how to find out the time in some cities of the world, when it is noon in London. The numbers show the number of hours ahead or behind London.

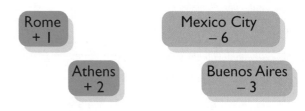

Use the 24-hour clock to answer the following questions.

   a What time is it in Athens when it is 10.00 in London?

   b What time is it in Rome, when it is noon in London?

   c What time is it in Mexico City when it is 14.00 in London?

   d What time is it in Athens when it is 09.00 in Buenos Aires?

   e What time is it in Rome when it is 10.00 in Mexico City?

2 **a** 4 times a number is 10 more than twice the number. Call the number x. Write down an equation and solve it to find x.

   b In tests, Yasmin scored half as many marks for history as she did for geography. She scored three times as many for history as she did for physics. If she scored m marks in physics, work out in terms of m how many she scored in history and geography. If she scored a total of 60 marks altogether how many did she score in each subject?

74

3 How much would 17 bookcases cost altogether, if each bookcase cost £45.00?

4 a A pair of shoes originally costing £80.00 were priced at £60.00 in a sale. What was the percentage reduction? (Remember, they now cost £60 out of the original £80.00.)

b In a swimming speed test, 80% of the candidates passed at their first attempt. 50% of the remainder passed on their second attempt. If there were 60 candidates originally, what percentage had not passed after their second attempt?

5 Harry buys a bar of chocolate which has 16 squares. He eats $\frac{1}{4}$ of the bar, and gives his friend half the squares that are left. His friend eats $\frac{2}{3}$ of the squares which Harry gave him, and then gives back to Harry half of the squares he has left. What fraction of the original bar does Harry now have? Give your answer in its lowest terms.

6 Study the diagrams.

Work out the lengths of the lines in the diagrams below, in terms of *d*, *e* and *f*.

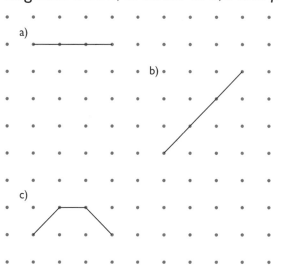

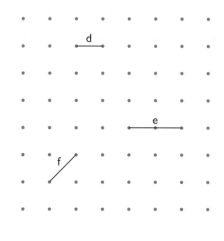

a)

b)

c)

d)

e)

7 In a tin of mixed biscuits, $\frac{1}{2}$ are plain, $\frac{1}{3}$ are chocolate and the other 10 are creams. How many biscuits are there in the tin?

8 a Rajah is warming up a meal in the microwave for his lunch, and has set the timer as shown. If the time now is 11.57, what time will the meal be ready?

b Harry has missed the bus back to afternoon school. The next bus is due at 13.13. How long does he have to wait?

9 In a class of students, 12 come to school by car, 8 walk and the other 4 cycle. What is the probability that one student chosen at random travels to school by car? Give your answer as a decimal.

10 The diagram shows a regular octagon JKLMNPQR. Angle JKL is 135°.

Work out the size of the following angles.

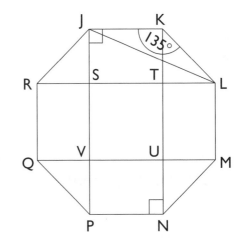

a ∠KJR

b ∠QPV

c ∠MUN

d ∠KJL

e What shape is STUV?

f What sort of triangle is triangle KTL?

11 In these magic squares every row, column and diagonal adds up to the same number.

a

7		
8	7	
		7

b

2		
	5	
	1	8

c

3	11	10
	5	

d

5	3	
	11	
	2	

What do you notice about the middle number and the total of each row, column and diagonal?

12 A teacher awarded stars for good work. Two red stars can be exchanged for one silver star. Three silver stars can be exchanged for one gold star. How many red stars would you need for one gold star?

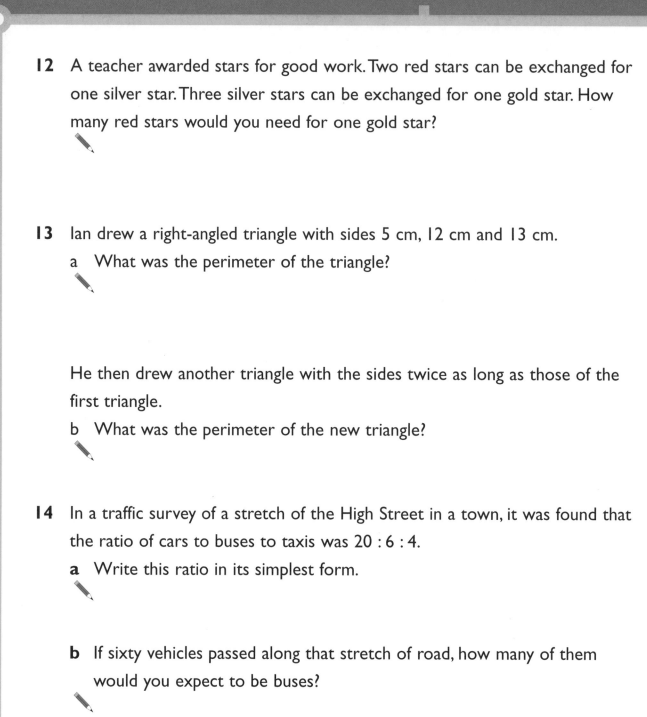

13 Ian drew a right-angled triangle with sides 5 cm, 12 cm and 13 cm.
a What was the perimeter of the triangle?

He then drew another triangle with the sides twice as long as those of the first triangle.
b What was the perimeter of the new triangle?

14 In a traffic survey of a stretch of the High Street in a town, it was found that the ratio of cars to buses to taxis was 20 : 6 : 4.
a Write this ratio in its simplest form.

b If sixty vehicles passed along that stretch of road, how many of them would you expect to be buses?

c Complete the following:

_____ times as many cars as taxis passed along the High Street.
d What fraction of the vehicles were cars?

15

a)

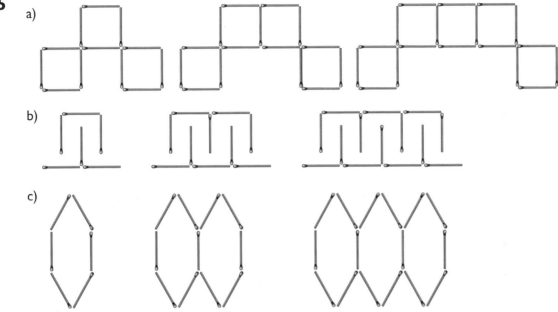

b)

c)

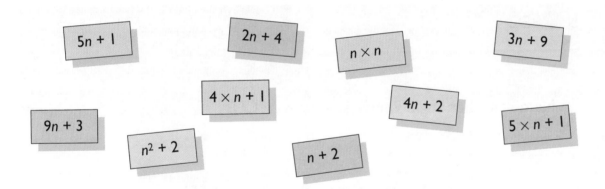

The number of matchsticks needed for making each pattern is given by its *n*th term. Match each card to its diagram. You will not need to use all the cards, but you may use some cards more than once.

5n + 1	2n + 4	n × n	3n + 9

4 × n + 1   4n + 2

9n + 3   5 × n + 1

n² + 2   n + 2

✎ The *n*th term of sequence a is _____ .

✎ The *n*th term of sequence b is _____ .

✎ The *n*th term of sequence c is _____ .

16 a Three bus routes start from the same garage. One bus runs every four minutes, one runs every five minutes and one runs every six minutes. They all leave the garage at 8.00 a.m. When is the next time that they all leave together? (**Hint**: Use the LCM.)

b A container, when it is full of sand, weighs 8 kg. The same container, when it is half full, weighs 5.2 kg. Find the weight of the container.

17 ABCD is a sketch of a square. EF is a line of symmetry and ∠FEC = 37°.
Find the size of the following angles.

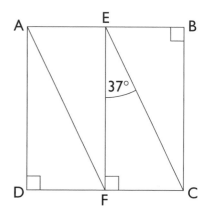

a ∠ECF

b ∠BEC

c Name another angle which is equal to ∠CEF.

d AB is 10 cm long. What is the area of triangle CEF?

e What name is given to the shape AECF?

18 A teacher said that anyone scoring less than 70% in a test would receive a detention. Helen scored 42 out of 56. Did she get a detention?

19 **a** 0.3×0.2

b $4.6 \div 20$

c Find the value of $100y$, if $y = 0.8$.

d Find the value of z if $50z = 1.5$.

20 Use only integers (whole numbers) to answer these questions.

a Jill drew a rectangle 4 cm by 3 cm.

i What was the area?

ii What was the perimeter? Remember to state your units.

b Anna drew a rectangle with the same area, but the perimeter was 16 cm. What were the length and width?

c Richard drew a different rectangle with the same area as those of Jill and Anna, but with a different perimeter. What were the length, width and perimeter of Richard's rectangle?

TEST PAPER 3

Time allowed: I hour

You **may** use a calculator to help you with any question on this paper.

1 **a** At noon on one Monday in January the temperature was 2 °C.
By midnight it had fallen six degrees. What was the temperature at
midnight?

b On Tuesday it was three degrees colder than it had been the night before
at midnight. What was the temperature at midnight on Tuesday?

c The temperature rose on Wednesday morning by six degrees.
What was the temperature then?

2

Using the lengths given in the diagrams above, work out the perimeter of
each of the following shapes.

a   **b**   **c**

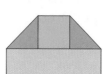   

3 Use your calculator to answer this question.

$$\frac{4.15 \times 6.2}{1.4 + 3.8}$$

Give your answer correct to 2 d.p.

4

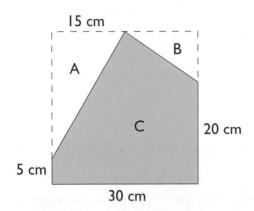

The diagram shows a pentagon which has been cut from a square of card of side 30 cm. (The rest of the square is indicated by the dotted lines.)

a What is the area of the square?

b What is the combined area of the two triangles?

c What is the area of the pentagon?

5 The width of a rectangle is t cm. It is three times as long as it is wide.

a Write the length of the rectangle, in cm, in terms of t.

b The perimeter of the rectangle is the same as twice the width plus 30 cm. Write an expression for the perimeter.

c Write an equation to show this information and use it to find the width of the rectangle.

6 **a** A farmer keeps cows and hens. If the number of legs is 12 more than twice the number of heads, how many cows does he have?

b Fill in the gap.

Mike has English homework every two days, Millie has English homework every five days and Mark has English homework every eight days. If they all have English homework on the first day of term, the next time that they will all have English homework is _____ days later.

7

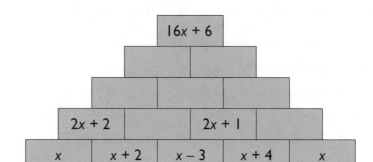

In this wall, the number on each brick is the sum of the two numbers below it. Fill in the missing numbers.

8 **a** Write these in order of size, starting with the smallest.

$$\frac{2}{3} \qquad \frac{4}{5} \qquad \frac{5}{6} \qquad \frac{3}{4} \qquad \frac{7}{9}$$

Hint: Change the fractions to decimals.

b $a = 1.73$ $b = 0.45$ $c = 5.64$

Work out the following, giving your answers to 2 d.p.

i $a - b$

ii ac

iii $(c + b) \times a$

iv $\dfrac{a + b}{c}$

9 This flower bed has a radius of 2.5 metres.
Mr Higgins wants to plant bedding plants round
the edge as shown.

    a What is the diameter of the bed?

    b What is the circumference of the bed? Give
       your answer in metres, correct to 1 d.p.

    c Rewrite your last answer in centimetres.

    d If he plans to plant four plants to every square metre, how many plants
       will he need?

    e He can only buy plants in trays of ten. How many trays does he need to
       buy?

10 Simplify the following.

    a $4t + 3t - 2t^2$

    b $4(2g + 7)$

    c $3r - 7r$

11 In a bag of 28 marbles, ten are blue, six are green and the rest are red. What is the probability (as a decimal correct to 2 d.p.) that one marble, chosen at random will be:

a blue

b red

c green or blue

d not blue.

12 JLNQ is a square. K is the midpoint of JL and P is the midpoint of QN. JR is one quarter the length of JQ and LM is one quarter the length of LN.

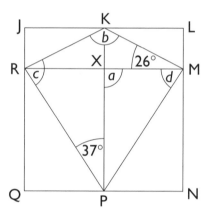

a Find the size of angles *a*, *b*, *c* and *d*.

b What name is given to the shape KMPR?

c Name a line of symmetry in the shape.

d What is the order of rotational symmetry of the shape KMPR?

e How many different triangles of different sizes are there in the shape?

13 Two classes were asked about their favourite sport.

In class 8A, 12 students out of 25 asked gave football as their favourite sport. Class 8G drew a pie chart to show their preferences. The angle that they drew to show the number who preferred football was 160°. Which class had the higher percentage of football lovers? You must show your working.

14 The diagram shows a square with a circle inside it.

The radius of the circle is *r* units.

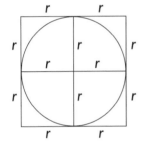

a Write an expression for the perimeter of the square.

b If *r* = 6 cm, work out the perimeter of this shape.

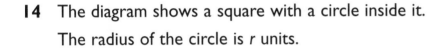

c If *r* = 10 cm work out the perimeter of this shape.

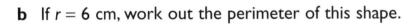

(**Hint**: What fraction of the circumference is the curved length?)

15 Find the area of a circle of diameter 10.6 m.

16 Use your calculator to find the cube root of 314 432.

17 Complete the magic squares.

a

-1	4	
	2	
	0	

b

2		
	3	6
		4

18 The interior angle of a regular hexagon is 120°. Do regular hexagons tessellate? Give a reason for your answer.

19 Solve the following equations.

a $2c + 10 = 14$

b $5d - 1 = 19$

c $c + 6 = 2$

d $3d + 2 = d + 16$

Bag 1   Bag 2

20 Answer the following questions. Where the question asks for a probability, give your answer as a decimal. Give the answers to all ratio questions in their simplest form.

a A disc is drawn from bag 1. What is the probability that it is red?

b A disc is drawn from bag 2. What is the probability that it is not red?

c Two discs are drawn from bag 1 and placed in bag 2. They are both blue. What is the probability that the next disc to be drawn from bag 1 is also blue?

d Bag 2 now includes the extra discs from bag 1. What is the probability that the next disc drawn from it is blue?

e All the discs are returned to their original bags. What is the ratio of red to blue discs in bag 1?

f What is the ratio of red to blue discs in bag 2?

g All the discs are now combined. What is the ratio of red to blue discs?

h Using the information from part g, complete the following sentence.

There are _____ times as many _____ discs altogether

as there are _____ discs.

ANSWERS

Answers to exercises

Number and algebra

Unit 1 Types of number

Exercise 1 (page 8)

1 6 Check: $4 \times 6 = 24$

2 13 Check: $30 - 17 = 13$

Exercise 2 (page 9)

1 81   2 390625

Unit 2 Factors and multiples

Exercise 1 (page 10)

1 $2^2 \times 3^2$

2 $2^4 \times 3$

3 3×5^2

4 $2^2 \times 3^2 \times 5$

Exercise 2 (page 11)

1 $40 = 2 \times 2 \times 2 \times 5$

$100 = 2 \times 2 \times 5 \times 5$

$HCF = 2 \times 2 \times 5 = 20$

2 $27 = 3 \times 3 \times 3$

$63 = 3 \times 3 \times 7$

$HCF = 3 \times 3 = 9$

Exercise 3 (page 12)

1 90   2 48   3 60

Exercise 4 (page 13)

$8 = 2 \times 2 \times 2$

$10 = 2 \times 5$

$12 = 2 \times 2 \times 3$

$LCM = 2 \times 2 \times 2 \times 3 \times 5 = 120$

They will leave together in 120 minutes = 2 hours' time at 12.00 noon.

Unit 3 Fractions, decimals and percentages

Exercise 1 (page 14)

1 $0.5 = \frac{5}{10} = \frac{1}{2}$ 2 $0.8 = \frac{8}{10} = \frac{4}{5}$

3 $0.75 = \frac{75}{100} = \frac{3}{4}$ 4 $0.32 = \frac{32}{100} = \frac{8}{25}$

Exercise 2 (page 15)

1 $\frac{3}{4} = 0.75 = 75\%$

2 $\frac{1}{5} = \frac{2}{10} = 0.2 = 20\%$

Unit 4 Working with fractions

Exercise 1 (page 16)

1 $\frac{3}{4}$ 2 $\frac{1}{4}$ 3 $\frac{1}{6}$

4 $\frac{7}{16}$ 5 $\frac{1}{3}$ 6 $\frac{1}{5}$

Exercise 2 (page 17)

1 $8\frac{7}{20}$ 2 $6\frac{5}{16}$

Exercise 3 (page 18)

1 $2\frac{3}{4}$ 2 $2\frac{11}{40}$

Exercise 4 (page 19)

1 $\frac{3}{11}$ 2 $\frac{15}{32}$

Exercise 5 (page 19)

1 $3\frac{3}{32}$ 2 15 (Remember, $\frac{15}{1} = 15$)

Exercise 6 (page 20)

1 $\frac{3}{8}$ 2 $\frac{5}{6}$

Exercise 7 (page 21)

1 2   2 $4\frac{4}{7}$

Exercise 8 (page 22)

1 $5\frac{5}{15}$ 2 $2\frac{7}{8}$ 3 $3\frac{3}{4}$ 4 $2\frac{7}{10}$

Unit 5 Multiplying and dividing decimals

Exercise 1 (page 24)

1 0.24   2 0.051

Exercise 2 (page 25)

1 2   2 120

Unit 6 Percentages

Exercise 1 (page 26)

1 a 50%   b 25%   c 45%   d 150%

2 a 75%

b $37\frac{1}{2}\%$ or 37.5% (38% to nearest 1%)

c 90%   d 35%

e $62\frac{1}{2}\%$ or 62.5% (63% to nearest 1%)

Exercise 2 (page 27)

1 a £7.50   b £19.20   c £54   d £252

2 a £40   b £280

Unit 7 Ratio

Exercise 1 (page 28)

1 $12:9 = 4:3$ 2 $24:18 = 12:9 = 4:3$

3 $36:15 = 12:5$ 4 $48:27 = 16:9$

Exercise 2 (page 29)

1 $2:1$ 2 $1:2$

3 $\frac{1}{3}$ 4 32

Unit 8 Positive and negative numbers

Exercise 1 (page 30)

1 6   2 4   3 0   4 −5

Exercise 2 (page 31)

1 3   2 8

3 −2   4 −2

Unit 9 Basics of algebra

Exercise 1 (page 34)

1 8   2 4   3 2   4 16

Exercise 2 (page 35)

1 a $4f + 2g$ b $6f + 3g$ c $4f + 4g$

d $12f + 3g$ e $6f + 5g$

2 a $3r + 3s$ b $6a$ c $x + y + 5xy$

d $5p + p^2 + pq$

Exercise 3 (page 36)

1 −9

Exercise 4 (page 36)

1 $x = 6$ 2 $y = 4$

ANSWERS

Exercise 5 (page 37)

1 $e + e + 15 + e - 5 = 220$
   $3e + 10 = 220$
   $3e = 210$
   $e = 70$ CDs

2 **a** $r + 4$ **b** $4(r + 4)$
   c $4(r + 4) = 56$
   There are several ways of solving the equation. If you have a different way, you can use it but remember to show your working.
   $4r + 16 = 56$
   $4r = 56 - 16 = 40$
   $r = 40 \div 4 = 10$ cm

Unit 10 Using equations

Exercise 1 (page 38)

1 $a = 5$ 2 $v = -4$ 3 $t = 0.5$ or $\frac{1}{2}$

Exercise 2 (page 39)

1 6 cm, 8 cm, 10 cm   2 12 years

Unit 11 Trial and improvement

Exercise 1 (page 40)

1 $x = 2.3$ 2 $x = 7.2$

Unit 12 Sequences

Exercise 1 (page 41)

1 8, 11, 14 … 155
2 1, 8, 15 … 344
3 −5, −4, −3 … 44

Unit 13 Mappings, equations and graphs

Exercise 1 (page 42)

a $y = x + 2$ **b** $y = x + 5$ **c** $y = x$

Exercise 3 (page 44)

1 It is always 6
2 It is always −8

Exercise 4 (page 45)

1 The lines get steeper and closer to the y axis.
2 The line gets shallower and closer to the x axis than $y = x$.

Shape, space and measures

Unit 14 How to label lines and shapes

Exercise 1 (page 48)

1 $180° - b = a$ 2 $180° - e = c + d$
3 $f = 180° \div 4 = 45°$ 4 $j + k + l = m + n$

Exercise 2 (page 49)

1 110° $(180° - \angle AED)$
2 360° (DEBC is a quadrilateral.)

Unit 15 Polygons

Exercise 1 (page 50)

1 4   2 2   3 5   4 6
5 8   6 Infinitely many

Exercise 2 (page 51)

1 90°
2 Each shape would be a trapezium.

Exercise 3 (page 52)

1 square, rectangle, parallelogram or rhombus
2 square, rhombus or kite
3 square or rectangle

Exercise 4 (page 53)

1 trapezium or parallelogram
2 rectrangle or rhombus
3 square

Exercise 5 (page 54)

1 rectangle or rhombus
2 parallelogram, kite and trapezium
3 square

Exercise 6 (page 55)

1 $p = 65°$ (opposite angles
   $q = 115°$ $(180° - 65°)$, $r = 57.5°$
   (It is one of the two equal angles of an isosceles triangle. $180° - 65° = 115°$.
   $\frac{1}{2}$ of $115° = 57.5°$)
2 If you are not sure, use a piece of tracing paper. You should find that the answer is E.
3 If you put a tracing of triangle C over triangle A, H or J it should fit exactly. They are all congruent.
4 rhombus
5 reflection

Unit 16 Enlargement

Exercise 1 (page 56)

1 15 cm   2 20 cm   3 60 cm

Exercise 2 (page 57)

1 AB′Y   2 AYB′

Unit 17 Circles

Exercise 1 (page 58)

1 7.9 cm   2 11.9 cm
3 44.6 cm   2 16.3 cm

Exercise 2 (page 59)

1 66.5 cm²   2 191.1 cm²
3 24.6 cm²   4 22.1 m²
5 6.6 m²

Unit 18 Area

Exercise 1 (page 60)

1 24 cm $\div$ 8 = 3 cm
2 24 cm² $\div$ 2 = 12 cm²
3 5 cm $(4 \times 5 \div 2 = 10)$

Exercise 2 (page 61)

1 9 cm   2 60 cm²   3 obtuse angled

ANSWERS

Unit 19 Area of composite shapes
Exercise 1 (page 62)
1 127.12 m   2 776.71 m²
Exercise 2 (page 63)
1 188.50 m   2 2313.72 m²

Handling data
Unit 20 Frequency diagrams
Exercise 1 (page 66)
1 18°   2 126°   3 15%
Exercise 2 (page 67)
1 America   2 8H
Exercise 3 (page 67)
1 18°   2 5%   3 20%

Unit 21 Scatter diagrams and correlation
Exercise 1 (page 68)
1 Negative correlation
2 Positive correlation
Exercise 2 (page 69)
1 Positive correlation.   2 i and n

Unit 22 Probability
Exercise 1 (page 70)
1 There are 36 possible outcomes, so the denominator will be 36. The number 6 occurs 5 times, so the answer is $\frac{5}{36}$.
2 The number 10 occurs 3 times, so the answer is $\frac{3}{36}$. This will cancel. $\frac{3}{36} = \frac{1}{12}$.
3 7. The probability is $\frac{1}{6}$.
Exercise 2 (page 71)
1 0.64   2 0.43   3 0.24
4 64%   5 128 meals

Answers to tests
Mental arithmetic test
1 2 cm   2 10   3 6   4 3
5 three million, nine hundred and ninety-nine thousand and two
6 500 ÷ 4 = 125. 125 × 3 = 375 cats
7 90° = $\frac{1}{4}$ of a circle, so it represents 15 students.
8 £40.50   9 6000
10 35   11 100 − 16 = 84
12 Each side is 6 cm, so the perimeter is 4 × 6 = 24 cm.
13 The radius = 4 m. Area is approximately 4² × 3 = 48 m².
14 3 × 5 + 1 = 16
15 5 × 4 ÷ 2 = 10 cm²
16 1 − 0.65 = 0.35
17 (15 − 1) ÷ 2 = 7
18 3500 m   19 6t   20 60

Test Paper 2
1 a 12.00   b 13.00   c 08.00
You will find **d** and **e** easier if you work out the time in London first.
   d 14.00   e 17.00
2 a $4x = 2x + 10$, $4x − 2x = 10$, $2x = 10$, $x = 5$
   b physics = m, history = $3m$, geography = $6m$
      $m + 3m + 6m = 60$
      $10m = 60$, $m = 6$
      physics 6, history 18, geography 36
3 £765.00
4 a £60.00 out of £80.00 = $\frac{3}{4}$ = 75%. The reduction was 100% − 75% = 25%.
   b 80% of 60 = 48, so 12 failed on their first attempt; 50% of 12 = 6
      The number remaining was 60 − 54 = 6, 6 out of 60 = 10%
5 $\frac{7}{16}$
6 a $3d$ or $d + e$ b $3f$ c $d + 2f$
   d $2d + e$ or $4d$ e $4d$
7 $\frac{1}{2} + \frac{1}{3} = \frac{3}{6} + \frac{2}{6} = \frac{5}{6}$, $\frac{1}{6}$ of the biscuits = 10, number of biscuits = 10 × 6 = 60
8 a 12.02
   b 16 minutes
9 $\frac{12}{24}$ = 0.5
10 a 135°   b 45°   c 90°
   d 22.5°   e square
   f right-angled isosceles triangle
11 a

7	6	8
8	7	6
6	8	7

b

2	9	4
7	5	3
6	1	8

c

3	11	10
15	8	1
6	5	13

d

5	3	10
11	6	1
2	9	7

Every row, column and diagonal has a total of 3 times the middle number.

12 1 gold = 3 silver
1 gold = 3 silver = 6 red

13 a 30 cm
  b 60 cm

14 a 10 : 3 : 2 **b** 60 ÷ 15 = 4, 4 × 3 = 12
  c 5 **d** $\frac{20}{30} = \frac{2}{3}$

15 a 3n + 9 **b** 4n + 2 **c** 5n + 1

16 a The LCM of 4, 5 and 6 is 60, so they will leave together 60 minutes later at 9.00 a.m.
  b Half the sand weighs 2.8 kg, so all the sand weighs 5.6 kg; the container weighs 8.0 kg − 5.6 kg = 2.4 kg.

17 a 53° **b** 53° **c** ∠AFE, ∠FAD or ∠BCE **d** 25 cm²
  e parallelogram

18 $\frac{42}{56}$ × 100 = 75%, so she escaped a detention.

19 a 0.06 **b** 0.23 **c** 80
  d 0.03

20 a 12 cm², 14 cm **b** 6 cm and 2 cm
  c 12 cm and 1 cm, perimeter = 26 cm

Test Paper 3

1 a −4° **b** −7° **c** −1°

2 a 3a + b + 2c **b** 4c **c** 2b + 4c

3 4.95 Remember that a calculator will always multiply or divide before adding or subtracting. If you were wrong, try again using brackets, like this.
$$\frac{(4.15 \times 6.2)}{(1.4 + 3.8)}$$

4 a 900 cm²
  b Area $A = \frac{1}{2} \times 25 \times 15$ cm² = 187.5 cm²,
  Area $B = \frac{1}{2} \times 15 \times 10$ cm² = 75 cm²,
  Area A + B = 262.5 cm²
  c 900 − 262.5 cm² = 637.5 cm²

5 a 3t cm
  b 2t + 30 cm
  c 2t + 6t = 2t + 30 (2t = twice the width, 6t = twice the length)
  8t = 2t + 30, 6t = 30, t = 5
  The width is 5 cm

6 a 6 cows. Start by making all the animals two legged, i.e. hens. How many legs must you give them to turn them into four legged animals? The 12 spare legs can be distributed in pairs to turn 2 legged into four-legged animals.
  b The LCM of 2, 5 and 8 is 40, so the missing word is 'forty'.

7

				16x + 6				
			8x + 1		8x + 5			
		4x + 1		4x		4x + 5		
	2x + 2		2x − 1		2x + 1		2x + 4	
x		x + 2		x − 3		x + 4		x

8 a $\frac{2}{3}$ $\frac{3}{4}$ $\frac{7}{9}$ $\frac{4}{5}$ $\frac{5}{6}$
  b i 1.25 **ii** 9.76
   iii 10.54 **iv** 0.39

9 a 5 m **b** 15.7 m **c** 1570 cm
  d 63 plants **e** 7 trays

10 a 7t − 2t² **b** 8g + 28 **c** −4r

11 a 0.36 **b** 0.43 **c** 0.57 **d** 0.64

12 a a = 90°,
   b = 180° − (2 × 26°) = 128°,
   c = 26° + (180° − (90° + 37°)) = 79°,
   d = 79° − 26° = 53°
  b kite **c** KP **d** 1 **e** 12

13 12 out of 25 = 12 ÷ 25 × 100 = 48%
160° out of 360° = 160 ÷ 360 × 100
= 44%
Class 8a had the higher percentage of football lovers.

14 a 8r
  b 30.8 cm (half the circumference + the diameter)
  c 35.7 cm

15 88.2 m² (to 1 d.p.)

16 68

17 a

−1	4	3
6	2	−2
1	0	5

b

2	8	−1
0	3	6
7	−2	4

18 Yes, 120° × 3 = 360°, so they will fit round a point without a gap.

19 a c = 2 **b** d = 4 **c** c = −4
  d d = 7

20 a 0.375 **b** 0.875 **c** 0.5
  d 0.9 **e** 3 : 5 **f** 1 : 7 **g** 1 : 3
  h There are 3 times as many blue discs altogether as there are red discs.

angle	amount or turn where two (or more) lines meet
area	the flat space occupied by a shape, or inside it
axis of symmetry	mirror line
axis (plural **axes**)	the vertical or horizontal line on a graph; the line that divides a symmetrical shape into two exact mirror images
biased	event which is more likely to give one outcome than another
common denominator	a number into which two or more numbers will divide exactly.
commutative	an operation where the order does not matter (Multiplication is commutative because $3 \times 2 = 2 \times 3$.)
congruent	identical
consecutive	following without a gap
consecutive numbers	numbers that follow on in order, e.g. 1, 2, 3, …
cube	a 3D solid with square faces
cuboid	a 3D solid with rectangular faces
decagon	a ten-sided polygon
digit	individual numeral in a number: 6 has one digit, 20 has two digits, as does 3.4
dividend	a number or quantity to be divided (In the example $6 \div 2$, six is the dividend.)
divisor	the number that is divided by (In the example $6 \div 2$, two is the divisor.)
edge	where two faces of a solid meet
equidistant	at the same distance from
equilateral	equal sided
evaluate	find the value
expression	two or more terms in a formula, e.g. $4n + 2$
exterior angle	the angle formed at a vertex (corner) outside a polygon if one side is extended
factor	a number that divides into another number or quantity exactly, e.g. 4 is a factor of 8
frequency	the number of times an event happens
frequency diagram	a diagram to show the frequency of an event, e.g. a bar chart
front elevation	the view of an object from the front
hexagon	a six-sided polygon
highest common factor	the largest number which will divide exactly into two or more numbers without giving a fractional answer or leaving a remainder
horizontal axis	the axis in a graph that goes across, usually the x-axis (The **horizon** is horizontal.)
integer	whole number
interior angle	the angle inside the vertex (corner) of a polygon
intersect	cross (Lines that cross each other are **intersecting lines**.)
intersection	the point where two lines cross
inverse process	a process that 'undoes' the previous process (Addition and subtraction are inverse processes, and multiplication and division are inverse processes.)
isosceles triangle	a triangle with two sides the same and two angles the same
lowest common denominator	the smallest number into which two or more denominators will divide, used when adding or subtracting fractions
lowest common multiple	the smallest number into which two or more numbers will divide, used to find the lowest common denominator
mean	the sum of all the values in a set of data, divided by the number of values in the set
median	the middle value of a set of data arranged in order from left to right, smallest to largest
modal group	the range of values that occurs most often (has the highest frequency) in a set of grouped data, e.g. ages 5–9

mode	the most common value in a given set (the value with the highest frequency)
multiple	a number with two or more factors, a number formed by multiplying two other numbers, e.g. 12 is a multiple of 3, 20 is a multiple of 10
net	a hollow 3D shape opened up and laid flat
numeral	single figure in a number, like a letter in a word
octagon	an eight-sided polygon
outcome	the result of an event in probability (Throwing a penny has two possible outcomes, head or tail.)
parallel	two (or more) lines that are always equidistant from each other (Spelling hint: The two letter Is in the word 'parallel' are parallel lines.)
parallelogram	a four-sided shape with one pair of opposite sides equal and parallel (In fact, both pairs are equal and parallel, but the proof will come in later years.)
pentagon	a five-sided polygon
perimeter	the distance all round a shape
perpendicular	meeting or intersecting at right angles (90°)
plan view	a view of an object looking down from above
polygon	a two-dimensional (2D), straight-sided shape with three or more sides
probability scale	a measure of probability, like a number line, from 0 to 1
product	the result of multiplying two numbers together
quadrant	a quarter of a graph grid (The x- and y-axes divide a graph into four quadrants.)
quadrilateral	a four-sided polygon
quotient	the result of dividing a number or amount by another number (In $6 \div 2 = 3$, the quotient is 3.)
random	by chance (A random sample is one in which all members of the group have equal chances of being chosen.)
range	the largest value minus the smallest value in a set of data
rhombus	a quadrilateral with all sides equal and opposite sides parallel and the diagonals cross at right angles.
sample	group of people taken as being typical, to take part in a survey
scale factor	the number by which every length of a shape is multiplied in an enlargement.
scalene triangle	triangle in which each side is a different length and all angles are different
sequence of numbers	a list of numbers that form a pattern according to a given rule
side elevation	the view of an object from the side
simplify	collect together all the same variables in an expression or equation, e.g. $1 + 2t + 1 + 3t + 2 = 5t + 4$
sum	the total of two or more numbers added together
survey	research, find out people's opinions by asking questions
term	a number in a sequence (The first number is the first term, the next is the second term, and so on.)
trapezium	a quadrilateral with one pair of sides parallel but unequal
unbiased	an event in which all outcomes have an equal chance of occurring
variable	numbers that do not necessarily have a fixed value, but vary, usually represented by letters in algebra
vertex	corner (The plural is **vertices**.)
vertical	upright
vertical axis	the axis in a graph that goes up and down the page, at right angles o the horizontal axis, and usually called the y-axis
vertices	corners, plural of **vertex**

INDEX